THE FABER LIBRARY—No. 28

UR OF THE CHALDEES

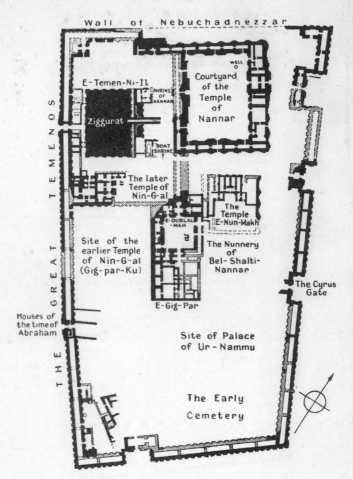

Plan of Ur

UR OF THE CHALDEES

*A Record of Seven Years
of Excavation*

by

C. Leonard Woolley

*Director of the Joint Expedition
of the British Museum and the
Museum of the University of
Pennsylvania to Mesopotamia*

London
Faber and Faber Limited
24 *Russell Square*

THIS NEW EDITION
IN THE FABER LIBRARY
FIRST PUBLISHED IN SEPTEMBER MCMXXXV
BY FABER AND FABER LIMITED
24 RUSSELL SQUARE LONDON
PRINTED IN GREAT BRITAIN
BY HENDERSON AND SPALDING LIMITED

CONTENTS

LIST OF ILLUSTRATIONS

List of Illustrations

MAPS

FOREWORD

IN THIS BOOK I HAVE ATTEMPTED TO DESCRIBE IN A popular form the work which during the last seven years has been done at Ur by the Joint Expedition of the British Museum and the Museum of the University of Pennsylvania. The results of the excavations have aroused very general interest, and it is in answer to requests from many quarters that I have undertaken this account.

The final publication of the results of such an expedition as this is necessarily a slow matter : one volume, that on al 'Ubaid, has already appeared, but some time must pass before other volumes are prepared for the Press. In the meantime there is a widespread desire for information. The annual reports are not accessible to everyone and are often too detailed for general readers, and newspaper accounts dealing with successive phases of the work are ephemeral and even in the mass give no connected picture. In my book *The Sumerians* I illustrated freely from our discoveries the history and achievements of the race now resuscitated from oblivion, but of the actual work of the expedition as carried on and of its results there has been no consecutive story told. This gap I have here tried to fill ; and though this small book does not in any way anticipate the official publications which will ultimately appear, does not in fact contain nearly all the material which has already figured in the reports in the *Antiquaries' Journal*, it may yet meet the needs of those who are interested in what the Expedition has already done and wish to follow with better understanding its future discoveries.

Rough Map showing the position of Ur in Sumeria.

INTRODUCTION

UR LIES ABOUT HALF-WAY BETWEEN BAGHDAD AND THE head of the Persian Gulf, some ten miles west of the present course of the Euphrates. A mile and a half to the east of the ruins runs the single line of railway which joins Basra to the capital of Iraq, and between the rail and the river there is sparse cultivation and little villages of mud huts or reed-mat shelters are dotted here and there ; but westwards of the line is desert blank and unredeemed. Out of this waste rise the mounds which were Ur, called by the Arabs after the highest of them all, the Ziggurat hill, ' Tell al Muqayyar,' the Mound of Pitch.

Standing on the summit of this mound one can distinguish along the eastern skyline the dark tasselled fringe of the palm-gardens on the river's bank, but to north and west and south as far as the eye can see stretches a waste of unprofitable sand. To the south-west the flat line of the horizon is broken by a grey upstanding pinnacle, the ruins of the staged tower of the sacred city of Eridu which the Sumerians believed to be the oldest city upon earth, and to the north-west a shadow thrown by the low sun may tell the whereabouts of the low mound of al 'Ubaid ; but otherwise nothing relieves the monotony of the vast plain over which the shimmering heat-waves dance and the mirage spreads its mockery of placid waters. It seems incredible that such a wilderness should ever have been habitable for man, and yet the weathered hillocks at one's feet cover the temples and houses of a very great city.

As long ago as 1854 Mr. J. E. Taylor, British Consul at Basra, was employed by the British Museum to investigate some of the southern sites of Mesopotamia, and chose for his chief work the Mound of Pitch. Here he unearthed inscriptions which for the first time revealed that the nameless ruin was none other than Ur, so-called ' of the Chaldees,' the home of Abraham. Taylor's discoveries were not at the time apprised at their true worth and his excavations closed down after two seasons ; but more and more the importance of the site came to be recognised, and though, partly through lack of funds and partly because of the lawless character of the district into which foreigners could penetrate only at their own risk, no further excavations were undertaken, yet the British Museum never gave up hope of carrying on the work which Taylor had begun.

Towards the end of the nineteenth century an expedition sent out by the University of Pennsylvania visited Ur and contrived to do a little excavation of which the results have never been published, and then again the site lay fallow until the Great War brought British troops into Mesopotamia and gave an opportunity for long-cherished hopes to be revived and realised. In 1918 Mr. R. Campbell Thompson, formerly assistant in the British Museum and then on the Intelligence Staff of the Army in Mesopotamia, excavated at Eridu and made soundings at Ur. The British Museum was encouraged to put a regular expedition into the field, and when Mr. Leonard King, who was to have led it, fell ill, Dr. H. R. Hall took his place and during the winter of 1918–19 dug at Ur, Eridu, and al 'Ubaid. Dr. Hall's work at Ur was of an experimental nature, richer in promise than fulfilment, but his expedition was of prime importance in that he discovered and partly excavated the little mound of al 'Ubaid with its remarkable remains of early architectural decoration.

Again the want of pence which vexes public institutions brought matters to a standstill. Then, in 1922, Dr. G. B. Gordon, Director of the University Museum of Pennsylvania, approached the British Museum with the proposal of a joint expedition to Mesopotamia ; the offer was accepted, and Ur was chosen as the scene of operations. The directorship of the Joint Expedition was entrusted to me, and now for seven winters in succession work has been carried on in the field, with what success this book is meant to show.

Ur of the Chaldees

Chapter I

The Beginnings of Ur, and the Flood

THE HISTORY OF UR GOES BACK FAR BEYOND THE FLOOD into those dim days when the Euphrates Valley, at least at its lower end, was still a great marsh through which the waters of the two rivers made their sluggish way to the sea. Gradually, as the streams brought down more and more silt from the north, the marsh land began to shrink, ' the waters were gathered together into one place, and the dry land appeared,' and from the uplands of Arabia or from the higher reaches of the middle Euphrates settlers drifted down to occupy such islands as gave a chance for men to live and cultivate the earth, that rich alluvial soil which as soon as it was free from the water would ' bring forth grass, the herb yielding seed, and the fruit tree yielding fruit after his kind, whose seed is in itself.'

One of these islands was Ur. Our excavations have not yet gone deep enough to lay bare more than a few scattered relics of the very early days, but at al 'Ubaid, about four miles from Ur, we have dug out part of such a primitive settlement. Here a little knoll, fortunately never covered afterwards with buildings, preserved the remains of huts constructed of mud and wattle or slight timber framing filled in with reed mats, with floors of beaten mud and fireplaces of mud or crude brick, and wooden doors whose hinge-poles turned on stone sockets.

In the ruins we found quantities of the fine painted hand-made pottery such as occurs in the lowest levels touched at Ur (Plate I *a*), rougher household wares used for cooking and storage, hoes and adzes of chipped and polished stone, saw-toothed flints and flakes of imported volcanic glass, sickles made of hard-baked clay (Plate I *b*), all the evidence of a very simple culture. It was clear that these people cultivated the soil and reaped their harvest of grain ; they kept domesticated cattle, sheep and goats ; they fished in the marshes (for we found fish-hooks and model boats), and, judging from fragments of painted terra-cotta figures of men and women, they seem to have painted or tatooed their bodies ; stone weights showed that the loom was known, so that they had advanced beyond the stage when men wore only the skins of beasts (though the tradition of such sheep-skin garments remained on into much later times) ; and for luxury they had beads cut from shell or rudely chipped from transparent white quartz, carnelian, and obsidian.

There was nothing to show to what race these first inhabitants of Mesopotamia belonged, but it is natural to connect them with the Semitic-speaking Akkadians whom later on we find occupying the northern half of the river-valley ; in any case we can see them as a primitive, not to say a barbarous people who, while they had certainly made some advance on the road to civilisation, were yet very far from being what we should term a civilised community.

At al 'Ubaid the settlement seems to have been comparatively short-lived ; at Ur a similar settlement but on a much larger scale must have endured for a very long time ; and as the frail mud huts fell into decay and over the ruins of them new huts were built, only to collapse and be built over in their turn, the ground-level rose, just as it does in any modern mud-built village of the Near East, and what had been a low island became a hill. Then, at a date which we cannot fix, people of a new race made their way into the valley, coming whence we do not know, and settled down side by side with the old inhabitants. These were the Sumerians.

Quoting probably some legend of the Sumerians

themselves, the Old Testament says that 'the people journeyed from the East and came into the plain of Shinar' (which is Babylon), 'and dwelt there,' and of recent years excavations so far away to the east as the valley of the Indus river have produced remains of an early civilisation which has certain elements in common with what we find in Mesopotamia. The Sumerians believed that they came into the country with their civilisation already formed, bringing with them the knowledge of agriculture, of working in metal, of the art of writing— 'since then,' said they, 'no new inventions have been made '—and if, as our excavations seem to show, there is a good deal of truth in that tradition, then it was not in the Euphrates valley that the arts were born, and though it is not likely to have been the Indus valley either, later research may well discover some site between those two extremes where the ancestors of our Sumerians developed the first real civilisation of which we have any knowledge.

At Ur, as elsewhere, the newcomers took over the old hill-village and rebuilt it as a town, putting up permanent buildings of burnt brick and surrounding it with stout walls of defence. The former inhabitants were not driven out, but, inferior as they were in all the arts of life, must have sunk to the condition of serfs. In the lowest levels which we have yet excavated we find their handiwork mixed up with that of the Sumerians, the old painted pottery side by side with the wheel-made clay pots and stone vessels of the higher civilisation, so that we can safely argue for a mixed population ; but just as the Norman castle from its hill dominated the low-lying village of the English villeins, so must we suppose that here the walled town was more or less reserved for the moral conquerors of the country, the Sumerians, while the ' barbarians ' put up their mud huts at the foot of the mound's slope or on the flat cultivated land. Many generations passed : the acropolis of Ur rose higher and higher into the air as the refuse of its houses was piled in the streets or flung out over its walls—and then came the Flood.

It has long been agreed that the story of the Flood as told in Genesis is based on the Sumerian legend, of which the oldest written versions that we possess go back more than two thousand years before Christ and are therefore some centuries older than Abraham, but many authorities have doubted whether either story had any basis in historical fact. That the Sumerians had no such doubt is clear, for, apart from the legend, overlaid as it is with mythology and miracle, the annalists in their sober table

of the reigns of kings made mention of it as an event
which interrupted the course of history : they
vouchsafe us no details about it—' then came the
Flood, and after the Flood kingship again descended
from heaven '—but since two or three Sumerian
cities are said to have existed equally before the
Deluge and after it, we may assume that the historical
break was not final, and that so far from the disaster
being universal some at least of the local centres of
civilisation survived it. Fuller references to the
Flood may yet be discovered on tablets buried in the
fertile soil of Mesopotamia, but even then some
might doubt whether these did more than amplify a
legend : the historian is apt to demand material
proof, and material proof of such an event as this is
very hard to find.

During the seasons 1927–8 and 1928–9 our work
on the prehistoric graveyard had resulted in the
excavation of a huge pit some 200 feet across and
between 30 and 40 feet deep. Now, practically the
whole of the soil which we had removed consisted of
household rubbish—the grey ashes from hearth
fires, black soot and half-burnt wood, grey mud
bricks decomposed and returned to their original
clay, burnt bricks broken or by the action of organic
salts reduced to red and yellow dust, masses of

potsherds, all in well-defined layers sloping steeply
down in one direction with holes and pockets
here and there which scarcely interrupted the
remarkable uniformity of the strata in general. At
the south-west end, where the ground rises to a high
mound, the slope of the rubbish-layers was more
pronounced and the more sharp the deeper we dug ;
to the north-east there was a gentler run, the strata
getting thicker as they went deeper, and low down
they became quite horizontal, and the sherds of
pottery which elsewhere had lain at all angles were
here flat and massed at the bottom of each layer,
while the soil in which they lay was smooth as if
water-laid and faded off at the top of each stratum
to a muddy black. It was into this rubbish that the
royal and other graves had been dug, and the rubbish
extended down below the graves.

There was only one explanation which would meet
the case. The rubbish was of course older, probably
much older, that the royal graves dug down into it,
ancient as they were ; the slope of the strata showed
that it was not the rubbish which accumulates in an
inhabited spot, for there the layers would lie horizontally, but had been thrown out as refuse, and it
had been thrown out from a height situated at the
south-west end of our excavation. The only height

from which refuse could so be thrown was the wall,
or the buildings, of the early town : the first rubbish
would be heaped against the wall ; what was emptied
over this would run down and form a talus, its slope
growing less steep as the foot of the pile spread
farther out ; with the rise in the level of the town
itself the mound too would rise, but always it would
stretch farther afield, and at last people would be
unable to pour out their refuse from the wall, because
the slope of the mound would be too gradual for it
to run down, and would be obliged to carry it out
and dump it on the mound's face : this would
account for the flattened layers at the north-east
end ; and the muddy strata with the pottery lying
horizontally proved that the rubbish mound ended
in a water-channel running parallel with the town
walls.   Led on by this, we made soundings beyond
the south-west end of our trench and found the
walls and floors of the primitive town.

Rubbish mounds 40 feet high must represent a
long period of time, a period certainly to be reckoned
in centuries, and with the excavation of the lowest
graves we were not yet at the bottom of the rubbish.
In the early spring of 1929, in the hopes of getting
some chronological evidence, we began sinking
shafts below the level of the deepest graves.

Almost at once discoveries were made which confirmed our previous views, if such confirmation were necessary : just below the floor of one of the royal tombs, in a layer of burnt wood ash, there were found numerous clay tablets inscribed with characters of a much more archaic type than those of the inscriptions in the graves. The discovery was made at the north-east end of the excavated area, where even the lowest rubbish would belong to a comparatively late period in the formation of the mound ; but as on the evidence of the writing the tablets might be assigned to about the thirty-seventh century before Christ—were, that is, two or three hundred years older than the tombs—we had a satisfactory chronology for this particular stratum, and of course the farther we dug at the same level towards the south-west the older would be the material we should encounter.

One point struck us as most important. However deep we dug into the rubbish and however much our work carried us back in time behind the period of the royal graves, the objects found in that rubbish, pottery and the like, were precisely the same as what was found in the tombs themselves. In other words, throughout the whole period represented by the growth of the refuse dumps (so far as we had penetrated into them) and by the early cemetery the material civilisation of the people, at least on its domestic side, had changed remarkably little ; such variations as we found, in the writing for instance, meant no more than the development which is to be expected in the course of centuries, but development along uniform lines by people of the same race. The wonderful civilisation illustrated by the contents of the graves, which I shall describe later, had always seemed to imply a long past behind it ; now we had proof of just such a steady growth as we had assumed.

The shafts went deeper, and suddenly the character of the soil changed. Instead of the stratified pottery and rubbish we were in perfectly clean clay, uniform throughout, the texture of which showed that it had been laid there by water. The workmen declared that we had come to the bottom of everything, to the river silt of which the original delta was formed, and at first, looking at the sides of the shaft, I was disposed to agree with them, but then I saw that we were too high up. It was difficult to believe that the island on which the first settlement was built stood up so much above what must have been the level of the marsh, and after working out the measurements I sent the men back to work to deepen the hole.

The clean clay continued without change—the sole object found in it was a fragment of fossilised bone which must have been brought down with the clay from the upper reaches of the river—until it had attained a thickness of a little over 8 feet. Then, as suddenly as it had begun, it stopped, and we were once more in layers of rubbish full of stone implements, flint cores from which the implements had been flaked off, and pottery.

But here there was a remarkable change. Some of the pottery was exactly like what we had been finding above the clay and in the tombs, but mixed with this there were bits of the hand-made painted ware which distinguishes the pre-Sumerian village of al 'Ubaid, while the numerous flint implements, which evidently were being manufactured on the spot, were similar to those from al 'Ubaid and further differentiated this from the higher strata where flints were very rarely to be found. The great bed of clay marked, if it did not cause, a break in the continuity of history : above it we had the pure Sumerian civilisation slowly developing on its own lines ; below it there was a mixed culture of which one element was Sumerian and the other of that al 'Ubaid type which seems to have nothing to do with the Sumerians but to belong to the race which inhabited the river-valley before the Sumerians came into it.

One object which lay with the flints and potsherds under the clay was of prime importance. It was a brick of burnt clay. Now, the ruins which we had previously excavated at Ur cover a period of more than two thousand five hundred years, and at every age when there was much building activity the type of brick employed shows some modification ; the standards of measure, the relative proportions of the bricks, change, often different clays are used, and one can generally recognise at a glance and nearly always confirm with a metre scale the date of any wall or isolated brick. But this brick was different from any we had ever seen. Certainly it belonged to a period of which we had had no experience hitherto, and in a curious way it gave the impression of being older than any brick we had seen ; but what it did conclusively prove was that in this age of mixed culture Ur was not like al 'Ubaid, a village of mud huts and reed shelters, but contained permanent buildings solidly constructed, the town of a civilised people.

We had long before this seen the meaning of our discovery. The bed of water-laid clay deposited against the sloping face of the mound, which extended from the town to the stream or canal at the north-east end, could only have been the result of a flood ; no other agency could possibly account for it. Inundations are of normal occurrence in Lower Mesopotamia, but no ordinary rising of the rivers would leave behind it anything approaching the bulk of this clay bank : 8 feet of sediment imply a very great depth of water, and the flood which deposited it must have been of a magnitude un-paralleled in local history. That it was so is further proved by the fact that the clay bank marks a definite break in the continuity of the local culture ; a whole civilisation which existed before it is lacking above it and seems to have been submerged by the waters.

Taking into consideration all the facts, there could be no doubt that the flood of which we had thus found the only possible evidence was the Flood of Sumerian history and legend, the Flood on which is based the story of Noah. A pit sunk 300 yards away to the north-west gave us the same bed of water-laid clay, with beneath it the same flints and coloured pottery of the non-Sumerian folk ; the next step was to test the higher part of the ancient town mound above the level which the clay formed as the receding waters deposited it against the mound's flank.

Time was short and only a small area could be

excavated, and that not to a depth which could be expected to yield cultural remains of the al 'Ubaid type unmixed with those of the later comers. But going down through successive levels of occupation marked by floors of burnt brick or of beaten mud lying one above the other and by the ruins of house walls, we did pass quite suddenly from strata containing nothing but purely Sumerian remains to others which yielded side by side with these the familiar painted clay pots and implements of flint and volcanic glass ; and tracing downhill the sloping layers of the rubbish we were able to prove that these mixed levels in the town site corresponded to the rubbish layers which underlay the clay bank : about sixteen feet below a brick pavement which we could with tolerable certainty date as being not later than 3200 B.C., we were down in the ruins of that Ur which existed before the Flood.

Work on a much larger scale must be done before we shall be able to describe in any detail the culture of the antediluvian age ; at present we have done little more than prove its existence. One point, however, deserves to be emphasised : in the ruins of the houses we found numerous lumps of hard clay which had been the stoppers of bottles or jars, and stamped on these were the impressions of the owners' seals ; there were no inscriptions, but designs sometimes of an elaborate geometrical character, sometimes with rows of animals shown walking in hilly country, the figures drawn with an astonishing liveliness and skill. It is probable that where seals were employed the art of writing was already known, so that we may not unreasonably hope to unearth written documents actually older than the Flood ; but in any case the carving of these seals with their combination of naturalism with formed style bespeaks a state of society well advanced on the road to civilisation properly so called.

So much for the facts. What, then, is to be built up on them ? The discovery that there was a real deluge to which the Sumerian and the Hebrew stories of the Flood alike go back does not of course prove any single detail in either of those stories. This deluge was not universal, but a local disaster confined to the lower valley of the Tigris and Euphrates, affecting an area perhaps 400 miles long and 100 miles across ; but for the occupants of the valley that was the whole world ! I have said that in all probability of the two races which inhabited together the lower valley the Sumerians were the city dwellers and the non-Sumerians lived in such open and low-lying villages as we found at al 'Ubaid : a flood great enough to account for the eight-foot bank of clay would certainly have drowned out those mud-hut villages ; it is conceivable that it might spare some at least of the Sumerian cities, perched high on their mounds and protected by walls of burnt brick.

According to Sumerian annals, some of the cities did survive ; and though Ur is not mentioned amongst them, the fact that it lay so high and the discovery of burnt brick in its ruins makes its survival quite possible. In this way we can explain what before was one of the great puzzles of South Mesopotamian archæology, the sudden and complete disappearance of the painted pottery which at one time seems to have been universally distributed over the southern sites. The people who made it, the older inhabitants of the country, were wiped out by the Flood, and the Sumerians who survived it were able not only to develop their own civilisation uncontaminated, as our excavations prove they did, but also to advance northward and occupy the empty lands, with the result that they who, according to their own tradition, were originally but settlers on the sea-coast of the Persian Gulf, are found when history opens to be masters of the delta for a distance of 200 miles from the sea.

Chapter II

The Graves of the Kings of Ur

I HAVE SAID THAT THE DISCOVERY OF THE EVIDENCE of the Flood was a result of the excavation of the royal tombs. The greater part of three seasons' work has been devoted to the clearing of the great cemetery which lay outside the walls of the old town and occupied the rubbish heaps piled up between them and the water-channel, and the treasures which have been unearthed from the graves during that time have revolutionised our ideas of the early civilisation of the world.

The cemetery (there are really two cemeteries, one above the other, but I am speaking now only of the lower and older) consists of burials of two sorts, the graves of commoners and the tombs of kings. Because the latter have yielded the richest works of art one is inclined to think of them alone, but the graves of the common folk, as well as being a hundred-fold as many in number, have also produced very fine objects, and have afforded precious evidence for the dating of the cemetery.

The tombs of the kings appear to be on the whole earlier in date than the graves of their subjects, and this not so much because they lie at a deeper level, for that might be explained as a natural precaution, the larger and richer graves being dug deeper as a protection against robbers, but because of their relative positions. It is a common sight to see in a Moslem graveyard the tomb of some local saint surmounted by its little domed chapel and the other graves crowded round this as close as may be, as if the occupants sought the protection of the holy man. So it is with the royal tombs at Ur. The older private graves are clustered round them, bordering on them but respecting their sanctity ; later it seems as if the visible monuments of the dead kings vanished and their memory faded, leaving only a vague tradition of this being holy ground, and we find the newer graves invading the shafts of the royal tombs and dug right down into them.

The private graves are found at very varying levels, partly perhaps because there was no regular standard of depth, partly because the ground surface of the cemetery was far from uniform ; but, generally speaking, the higher graves are the later, and this is due to the rise in the ground-level, which went on steadily throughout the time that the graveyard was in use. The result of this rise obliterating the position of the older graves was that a new grave might be placed directly above an old but, being started from a higher level, would not go quite so far down, and we may find as many as half a dozen graves superimposed one above the other. When this is so, the position in the ground necessarily corresponds to the order in time, and from these superimposed graves we get most valuable evidence for chronology.

Judging from the character of their contents, pottery, etc., the later graves seem to come just before the beginning of the First Dynasty of Ur (*vide* Chapter III), which we date to about 3100 B.C., and a few are actually contemporary with that dynasty; for the cemetery age as a whole I think that we must allow a period of at least 300 years. The first of the royal tombs, then, may be dated soon after 3500 B.C., and soon after 3200 B.C. the graveyard was falling out of use. There is not space here to go into all the arguments, but everyone, I think, will agree that some time must have elapsed before the kings, buried as they were with such ghastly pomp, could be forgotten and the sanctity of the tomb-shafts be invaded by the common dead; and if we find above them six or more superimposed burials, between each of which there must have been a decent lapse of time, and the topmost of these dates before 3100 B.C., then the chronology which I suggest will not seem exaggeratedly long.

Often the first sign that the workmen have of a
grave as they dig down into the mixed soil of the
cemetery is a paper-thin wavy line of white powder
or else a few small holes set in a line and running
vertically into the earth ; either of these means the
abandonment of pick and spade and the careful use
of excavating knives. The holes are left by the
decay of the wooden staves which strengthened the
sides of a wooden or wickerwork coffin, the wavy
white line is the edge of the reed mat which lined
the grave or in which the bodies of poorer folk were
wrapped. It is an astonishing thing that in soil
wherein so much that seems enduring decays
entirely, a fragile thing like a piece of matting, though
it lose all its substance and can be blown away with
a breath, yet retains its appearance and its texture
and can with care be exposed in such condition
that a photograph of it looks like one of the real
matting which perished 5,000 years ago. So too
with wood ; nothing of it survives, but on the soil
there is left an impression, a cast as it were, which
with its effect of grain and colour might deceive the
eye, though a touch of the finger obliterates it more
easily than it dislodges the plumage from the wing
of a butterfly.

The ordinary grave consisted of a rectangular pit ;

at the bottom of this the body might be laid wrapped up in a roll of matting secured by a long copper pin ; or the dead man might be placed in a coffin, usually of wood or wickerwork, sometimes of clay. In either case we find with the body such personal belongings as beads and ear-rings, a knife or dagger, the pins that fastened the dress, and perhaps the cylinder seal the impression of which on a clay tablet was equivalent to the owner's signature. Outside the coffin or the matting roll were set what were more properly offerings to the dead, food and drink in vessels of clay, copper, or stone, weapons and tools ; in most cases mats lined the bottom of the pit and were laid over the offerings to keep them from immediate contact with the earth which was thrown back to fill the grave. The body lies always on its side, the legs slightly bent at hip and knee in the attitude of one asleep, and the hands are brought up before the face and hold close to the mouth a cup which must once have contained water. There does not seem to be any fixed rule for the direction of the body, no such orientation as is practised in Christian and Moslem lands to-day, and the graves often lie at right angles with their neighbours ; only the attitude of the body in the grave is constant.

The provision made for the dead seems clearly to prove a belief in a future life of some sort, but there is nothing found which expressly defines such belief ; in no single grave has there been any figure of a god, any symbol or ornament that strikes one as being of a religious nature ; the dead man took with him what he might require for a journey to or for a sojourn in another world, but what he thought about the world to which he was going nothing tells us On the other hand, the material life of the people is illustrated to a wonderful degree by the contents of their graves, and even had there been no royal tombs with their wealth of artistic treasures, we should have been able to obtain from the cemetery a very detailed knowledge of the civilisation of the age.

As we are dealing here with a period of which previously nothing was known, every object is in the nature of an historic monument, and a poor grave may contain something which while not intrinsically valuable is historically most precious. Thus last winter there was found standing by the side of a clay coffin robbed in antiquity and empty a painted clay vase of a type which had never before occurred in the whole of our cemetery work or indeed in the course of our excavations at Ur. Unique here, it would have been thoroughly at home in the prehistoric levels at Susa, far away in Persia, and being found where it was proved some intercourse between Persia and Ur towards the close of the cemetery period ; either some Persian immigrant had been buried here or the native owner of the imported vase had determined to take it with him to the grave.

As soon as a grave is detected, the workman concerned reports to the foreman and is instructed how to proceed. The first objects to be exposed are usually the clay pots, because these, if not crushed by the weight of the earth, stand higher than the other objects in the pit's bottom. Next the position of the body has to be ascertained—not always an easy matter, since the bones are often so decayed that only a difference in the colour of the soil betrays their presence ; and then the outline of the original grave-shaft is traced and the earth gradually removed from its whole area, only that round and over the head being left, as here if anywhere the more precious objects will be found. If anything of importance appears, gold or silver or beads, the workman must again stop work and report, and then one of the staff takes over the task of excavation. Nothing must be disturbed until the grave has been finally cleared, written up, drawn and photographed if necessary ; beads, if there are any, have to be noted in such wise that they can be re-strung in their original order, so as to reproduce the fashion of the time ; the skull, should it chance to be unusually well preserved, has to be treated with hot paraffin wax and removed for study at home ; the position of the grave is recorded on the plan ; and then, when nothing of it is left, pick and spade start again and work is carried down to a deeper level, where more and earlier graves await discovery.

Excavation of this sort is essentially a work of destruction ; in the early cemetery and in the cemetery of the Sargonid age which lay immediately above it we have dug and noted more than 1,400 private graves, and in the great yawning pit which is all our work has produced not a vestige of one of these remains, only, at the pit's bottom, the standing masonry of six royal tombs and the outlines, broken and irregular, of the death-pits. All the more care, therefore, must be taken to collect at once all the evidence that a grave may afford, even if its bearing be not immediately clear, for there is no going back later to repair omissions, and on the thoroughness of the note-taking more than on the importance of the objects depends the ultimate value of our work.

The routine of digging private graves may become

wearisome, for there is a great deal of repetition and only too many of the graves contain nothing of very obvious interest, though sometimes one is found which by its contents atones for a whole series wherein original poverty or subsequent plundering has disappointed our hopes. More than half the graves have been plundered. During the later part of the time when the cemetery was in use the diggers of the new graves, encountering one of an older day, could not resist the temptation to remove its more valuable contents; at a still later date there was building over the forgotten graveyard, and men employed in making foundations or laying drains made chance discoveries which encouraged them to more deliberate efforts. Sometimes the robbers must have had knowledge of the whereabouts of the tombs of the old kings but feared to attack them openly, for we have found circular shafts driven deep down into the level of the old graves and then turning horizontally to tunnel in the direction of a royal tomb : in some cases they have succeeded all too well ; in one or two they missed their mark and abandoned the attempt in disgust ; but at Ur, as in Egypt, tomb-robbing is an ancient profession, and we to-day are lucky if we hit upon a grave at once wealthy and intact.

The first of the royal tombs proved a disappointment. At the very end of the season 1926–7 two
important discoveries were made. At the bottom
of an earth shaft, amongst masses of copper weapons,
there was found the famous gold dagger of Ur, a
wonderful weapon whose blade was of gold, its hilt
of lapis lazuli decorated with gold studs, and its
sheath of gold beautifully worked with an openwork
pattern derived from plaited grass (Plate IV *b*);
with it was another object scarcely less remarkable,
a cone-shaped reticule of gold ornamented with
a spiral pattern and containing a set of little toilet
instruments, tweezers, lancet, and pencil, also of
gold. Nothing like these things had ever before come
from the soil of Mesopotamia; they revealed an
art hitherto unsuspected and they gave promise
of future discoveries outstripping all our hopes.

The other discovery was less sensational. Digging
down in another part of the cemetery we found what
at first appeared to be walls of *terre pisée*, i.e.
of earth not moulded into bricks but used as con-
crete is used for building. As the sun dried the soil
and brought out the colours of its stratification, it
became evident that these were no built walls but
the clean-cut sides of a pit sunk in the rubbish; the
looser filling of the pit had fallen away as we worked

and had left the original face exactly as the first diggers had made it. As the excavation continued we came on slabs and blocks of rough limestone which seemed to form a paving over the pit's base. This was an astonishing thing, because there is no stone in the Euphrates delta, not so much as a pebble in its alluvium, and to obtain blocks of limestone such as these it is necessary to go some thirty miles away into the higher desert. The cost of transport would be considerable, and the result is that stone is scarcely ever found in buildings at Ur : a stone pavement underground would therefore be an unheard of extravagance. As the season was just at its end we could do no more than clear the surface of the ' pavement ' and leave its fuller examination for the next autumn.

Thinking the matter over during the summer, we came to the conclusion that the stones might be not the floor of a building but its roof, and that we might have discovered a royal grave. It was with high hopes that we resumed work in the following autumn and very soon we could assure ourselves that our forecast was correct : we had found a stone-built underground structure which had indeed been the tomb of a king, but a rubbish-filled tunnel led from near the surface to the broken roof, robbers had been there before us, and except for a few scattered fragments of a gold diadem and some decayed copper pots there was nothing left for us to find.

But in spite of that disappointment the discovery was most important. We had laid bare the ruins of a two-chambered structure built of stone throughout with one long and narrow chamber vaulted with stone and a square room which had certainly once been covered with a stone dome, though the collapse of the roof made it difficult to establish the exact method of construction. A doorway, blocked with rubble masonry, afforded entrance to the tomb and was approached by a slanting ramp cut down from the ground surface in the hard soil. Nothing of the sort had ever been found before, and the light thrown on the architectural knowledge of this remote period might well atone for the loss of the tomb's contents ; moreover, there was no reason to suppose that this was an isolated tomb, and we could hope for others to which the plunderers had not made their way.

During that season (1927–8) and in the course of last winter more royal tombs came to light, and it is curious to find that never more than two of them are alike. Two large tombs, both plundered, consist of a four-roomed building occupying the whole area of

the excavated shaft at the bottom of which they lie ;
walls and roofs alike are of limestone rubble, and in
each case there are two long outer chambers which
are vaulted and two smaller central chambers
crowned with domes ; a ramp leads to the arched
door in the outer wall, and arched doors give com-
munication between the rooms. Two graves,those of
Queen Shub-ad and her supposed husband (Plate II),
consist of a pit open to the sky and approached by a
sloped ramp, at one end of which is a single-chamber
tomb with limestone walls and a roof constructed
of burnt brick, vaulted and with apsidal ends ; the
chamber was destined to receive the royal body, the
open pit was for offerings and subsidiary burials,
and was simply filled in with earth. In another case
the pit was found, but the tomb chamber did not lie
inside it, but seems to have been close by and on a
different level. A small grave found last winter
consists of a single stone-built domed chamber with
a little front court at the bottom of the shaft and,
higher up in the shaft, mud-brick buildings for the
subsidiary burials and offerings, the whole being
covered with earth ; another has the same general
arrangement, but instead of the domed stone
chamber there was a vaulted chamber of mud brick.

There is variety enough therefore in the actual

structures, but underlying all there was a common
ritual for which different generations provided in
different ways ; what that ritual was can best be
explained by describing the excavation of the graves.

In 1927–8, soon after our disappointment with the
plundered stone tomb, we found, in another part of
the field, five bodies lying side by side in a shallow
sloping trench ; except for the copper daggers at
their waists and one or two small clay cups they had
none of the normal furniture of a grave, and the
mere fact of there being a number thus together was
unusual. Then, below them, a layer of matting was
found, and tracing this along we came to another
group of bodies, those of ten women carefully
arranged in two rows ; they wore head-dresses of
gold, lapis lazuli, and carnelian, and elaborate bead
necklaces, but they too possessed no regular tomb
furnishings. At the end of the row lay the remains of
a wonderful harp, the wood of it decayed but its
decoration intact, making its reconstruction only a
matter of care ; the upright wooden beam was
capped with gold, and in it were fastened the gold-
headed nails which secured the strings ; the sounding-box was edged with a mosaic in red stone, lapis
lazuli, and white shell, and from the front of it projected a splendid head of a bull wrought in gold with

eyes and beard of lapis lazuli ; across the ruins of the harp lay the bones of the gold-crowned harpist.

By this time we had found the earth sides of the pit in which the women's bodies lay and could see that the bodies of the five men were on the ramp which led down to it. Following the pit along, we came upon more bones which at first puzzled us by being other than human, but the meaning of them soon became clear. A little way inside the entrance to the pit stood a wooden sledge chariot decorated with red, white, and blue mosaic along the edges of the framework and with golden heads of lions having manes of lapis lazuli and shell on its side panels ; along the top rail were smaller gold heads of lions and bulls, silver lionesses' heads adorned the front, and the position of the vanished swingle-bar was shown by a band of blue and white inlay and two smaller heads of lionesses in silver. In front of the chariot lay the crushed skeletons of two asses with the bodies of the grooms by their heads, and on the top of the bones was the double ring, once attached to the pole, through which the reins had passed ; it was of silver, and standing on it was a gold ' mascot ' in the form of a·donkey most beautifully and realistically modelled.

Close to the chariot were an inlaid gaming-

board * and a collection of tools and weapons, including
a set of chisels and a saw made of gold, big bowls of
grey soapstone, copper vessels, a long tube of gold
and lapis which was a drinking-tube for sucking up
liquor from the bowls, more human bodies, and
then the wreckage of a large wooden chest adorned
with a figured mosaic in lapis lazuli and shell which
was found empty but had perhaps contained such
perishable things as clothes. Behind this box were
more offerings, masses of vessels in copper, silver,
stone (including exquisite examples in volcanic
glass, lapis lazuli, alabaster, and marble), and
gold (Plate III, *b, c*) ; one set of silver vessels
seemed to be in the nature of a communion-
service, for there was a shallow tray or platter,
a jug with tall neck and long spout such as we
know from carved stone reliefs to have been used
in religious rites, and tall slender silver tumblers
nested one inside another ; a similar tumbler in
gold, fluted and chased, with a fluted feeding-bowl,
a chalice, and a plain oval bowl of gold lay piled
together, and two magnificent lions' heads in silver,
perhaps the ornaments of a throne, were amongst the
treasures in the crowded pit. The perplexing thing

* A more elaborate example of a gaming-board is figured
on Plate VI *b*.

was that with all this wealth of objects we had found no body so far distinguished from the rest as to be that of the person to whom all were dedicated ; logically our discovery, however great, was incomplete.

The objects were removed and we started to clear away the remains of the wooden box, a chest some 6 feet long and 3 feet across, when under it we found burnt bricks. They were fallen, but at one end some were still in place and formed the ring-vault of a stone chamber. The first and natural supposition was that here we had the tomb to which all the offerings belonged, but further search proved that the chamber was plundered, the roof had not fallen from decay but had been broken through, and the wooden box had been placed over the hole as if deliberately to hide it. Then, digging round the outside of the chamber, we found just such another pit as that 6 feet above (Plate II). At the foot of the ramp lay six soldiers, orderly in two ranks, with copper spears by their sides and copper helmets crushed flat on the broken skulls ; just inside, having evidently been backed down the slope, were two wooden four-wheeled waggons each drawn by three oxen—one of the latter so well preserved that we were able to lift the skeleton entire ; the waggons were plain,

but the reins were decorated with long beads of lapis
and silver and passed through silver rings surmounted with mascots in the form of bulls ; the grooms
lay at the oxen's heads and the drivers in the bodies
of the cars ; of the cars themselves only the impression of the decayed wood remained in the soil, but so
clear was this that a photograph showed the grain
of the solid wooden wheel and the grey-white
circle which had been the leather tyre.

Against the end wall of the stone chamber lay the
bodies of nine women wearing the gala head-dress of
lapis and carnelian beads from which hung golden
pendants in the form of beech-leaves, great lunate
ear-rings of gold, silver ' combs ' like the palm of
a hand with three fingers tipped with flowers whose
petals are inlaid with lapis, gold, and shell, and
necklaces of lapis and gold ; their heads were leaned
against the masonry, their bodies extended on to the
floor of the pit, and the whole space between them
and the waggons was crowded with other dead,
women and men, while the passage which led along
the side of the chamber to its arched door was lined
with soldiers carrying daggers, and with women. Of
the soldiers in the central space one had a bundle of
four spears with heads of gold, two had sets of four
silver spears, and by another there was a remarkable

PLATE I

(a) Painted pottery of the period before the Flood.

(b) Flint implements and clay models of tools from before
the Flood.

PLATE II

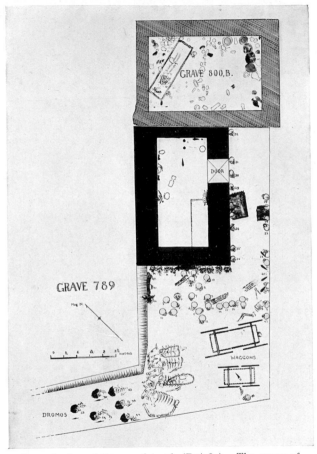

Ground plan of the royal tomb (Pg/789). The grave of
King A-bar-gi. The bodies of the human victims,
waggons, etc., are shown in position. The chamber
above (Pg 800) is that of Queen Shub-ad.

relief in copper with a design of two lions trampling on the bodies of two fallen men which may have been the decoration of a shield.

On the top of the bodies of the ' court ladies ' against the chamber wall had been placed a wooden harp, of which there survived only the copper head of a bull and the shell plaques which had adorned the sounding-box ; by the side wall of the pit, also set on the top of the bodies, was a second harp with a wonderful bull's head in gold, its eyes, beard, and horn-tips of lapis, and a set of engraved shell plaques not less wonderful ; there are four of them with grotesque scenes of animals playing the parts of men, and while the most striking feature about them is that sense of humour which is so rare in ancient art, the grace and balance of the design and the fineness of the drawing make of these plaques one of the most instructive documents that we possess for the appreciation of the art of early Sumer.

Inside the tomb the robbers had left enough to show that it had contained bodies of several minor people as well as that of the chief person, whose name, if we can trust the inscription on a cylinder seal, was A-bar-gi ; overlooked against the wall we found two model boats, one of copper now hopelessly decayed, the other of silver wonderfully well

D

preserved (Plate III *a*) ; some 2 feet long, it has high stern and prow, five seats, and amidships an arched support for the awning which would protect the passenger, and the leaf-bladed oars are still set in the thwarts ; it is a testimony to the conservatism of the East that a boat of identical type is in use to-day on the marshes of the Lower Euphrates, some 50 miles from Ur.

The king's tomb-chamber lay at the far end of his open pit ; continuing our search behind it we found a second stone chamber built up against it either at the same time or, more probably, at a later period. This chamber, roofed like the king's with a vault of ring arches in burnt brick, was the tomb of the queen to whom belonged the upper pit with its ass chariot and other offerings : her name, Shub-ad, was given us by a fine cylinder seal of lapis lazuli which was found in the filling of the shaft a little above the roof of the chamber and had probably been thrown into the pit at the moment when the earth was being put back into it. The vault of the chamber had fallen in, but luckily this was due to the weight of earth above, not to the violence of tomb-robbers ; the tomb itself was intact (Plate II).

At one end, on the remains of a wooden bier, lay the body of the queen, a gold cup near her hand ;

the upper part of the body was entirely hidden by a mass of beads of gold, silver, lapis lazuli, carnelian, agate, and chalcedony, long strings of which, hanging from a collar, had formed a cloak reaching to the waist and bordered below with a broad band of tubular beads of lapis, carnelian, and gold : against the right arm were three long gold pins with lapis heads and three amulets in the form of fish, two of gold and one of lapis, and a fourth in the form of two seated gazelles, also of gold.

The head-dress whose remains covered the crushed skull was a more elaborate edition of that worn by the court ladies : its basis was a broad gold ribbon festooned in loops round the hair—and the measurement of the curves showed that this was not the natural hair but a wig padded out to an almost grotesque size ; over this came three wreaths, the lowest, hanging down over the forehead, of plain gold ring pendants, the second of beech leaves the third of long willow leaves in sets of three with gold flowers whose petals were of blue and white inlay ; all these were strung on triple chains of lapis and carnelian beads. Fixed into the back of the hair was a golden ' Spanish comb ' with five points ending in lapis-centred gold flowers. Heavy spiral rings of gold wire were twisted into the side curls of the wig, huge lunate ear-rings of gold hung down to the shoulders, and apparently from the hair also hung on each side a string of large square stone beads with, at the end of each, a lapis amulet, one shaped as a seated bull and the other as a calf. Complicated as the head-dress was, its different parts lay in such good order that it was possible to reconstruct the whole and exhibit the likeness of the queen with all her original finery in place.

For the purposes of exhibition a plaster cast was made from a well-preserved female skull of the period (the Queen's own skull was too fragmentary to be used), and over this my wife modelled the features in wax, making this as thin as possible so as not to obliterate the bone structure ; the face was passed by Sir Arthur Keith, who has made a special study of the Ur and al 'Ubaid skulls, as reproducing faithfully the character of the early Sumerians. On this head was put a wig of the correct dimensions dressed in the fashion illustrated by terra-cotta figures which, though later in date, probably represent an old tradition. The gold hair-ribbon had been lifted from the tomb without disturbing the arrangement of the strands, these having been first fixed in position by strips of glued paper threaded in and out between them and by wires twisted round the gold ;

when the wig had been fitted on the head, the hair-ribbon was balanced on the top and the wires and paper bands were cut, and the ribbon fell naturally into place and required no further arranging. The wreaths were re-strung and tied on in the order noted at the time of excavation. Though the face is not an actual portrait of the queen, it gives at least the type to which she must have conformed, and the whole reconstructed head presents us with the most accurate picture we are likely ever to possess of what she looked like in her lifetime.*

By the side of the body lay a second head-dress of a novel sort. On to a diadem made apparently of a strip of soft white leather had been sewn thousands of minute lapis-lazuli beads, and against this background of solid blue were set a row of exquisitely fashioned gold animals, stags, gazelles, bulls, and goats, with between them clusters of pomegranates, three fruit hanging together shielded by their leaves, and branches of some other tree with golden stems and fruit or pods of gold and carnelian, while gold rosettes were sewn on at intervals, and from the lower border of the diadem hung palmettes of twisted gold wire.

* This head, with different wig and head-dress, is shown on Plate V.

The bodies of two women attendants were crouched against the bier, one at its head and one at its foot, and all about the chamber lay strewn offerings of all sorts, another gold bowl, vessels of silver and copper, stone bowls and clay jars for food, the head of a cow in silver, two silver tables for offerings, silver lamps, and a number of large cockle-shells containing green paint ; such shells are nearly always found in women's graves, and the paint in them, presumably used as a cosmetic, may be white, black, or red, but the normal colour is green. Queen Shub-ad's shells were abnormally big, and with them were found two pairs of imitation shells, one in silver and one in gold, each with its green paint.

The discovery was now complete and our earlier difficulty was explained : King A-bar-gi's grave and Queen Shub-ad's were exactly alike, but whereas the former was all on one plane, the queen's tomb-chamber had been sunk below the general level of her grave-pit. Probably they were husband and wife : the king had died first and been buried, and it had been the queen's wish to lie as close to him as might be ; for this end the grave-diggers had reopened the king's shaft, going down in it until the top of the chamber vault appeared ; then they had

stopped work in the main shaft but had dug down
at the back of the chamber a pit in which the queen's
stone tomb could be built. But the treasures known
to lie in the king's grave were too great a temptation
for the workmen ; the outer pit where the bodies
of the court ladies lay was protected by 6 feet of
earth which they could not disturb without being
detected, but the richer plunder in the royal
chamber itself was separated from them only by the
bricks of the vault ; they broke through the arch,
carried off their spoil, and placed the great clothes-
chest of the queen over the hole to hide their sacrilege.

Nothing else would account for the plundered
vault lying immediately below the untouched grave
of the queen, and the connecting of Shub-ad's stone
chamber with the upper ' death-pit,' as we came
to call these open shafts in which the subsidiary
bodies lay, made an exact parallel to the king's
grave and, in a lesser degree, to the other royal
tombs. Clearly, when a royal person died, he or she
was accompanied to the grave by all the members of
the court : the king had at least three people with
him in his chamber and sixty-two in the death-pit ;
the queen was content with some twenty-five in all.
Here we had a single stone chamber and an open
death-pit ; where there was a larger stone building

with two or four rooms, then one of these was for the royal body and the rest for the followers sacrificed in precisely the same way ; the ritual was identical, only the accommodation for the victims differed in different cases.

On the subject of human sacrifice more light was thrown by the discovery of a great death-pit excavated last winter. At about 26 feet below the surface we came upon a mass of mud brick not truly laid but rammed together and forming, as we guessed, not a floor but the stopping, as it were, of a shaft. Immediately below this we were able to distinguish the clean-cut earth sides of a pit, sloping inwards and smoothly plastered with mud ; following these down, we found the largest death-pit that the cemetery has yet produced. The pit was roughly rectangular and measured 27 feet by 24 at the bottom, and was approached as usual by a sloped ramp. In it lay the bodies of six men-servants and sixty-eight women ; the men lay along the side by the door, the bodies of the women were disposed in regular rows across the floor, every one lying on her side with legs slightly bent and hands brought up near the face, so close together that the heads of those in one row rested on the legs of those in the row above. Here was to be observed even more clearly what had been fairly obvious in the graves of Shub-ad and her husband, the neatness with which the bodies were laid out, the entire absence of any signs of violence or terror.

We have often been asked how the victims in the royal graves met their death, and it is impossible to give a decisive answer. The bones are too crushed and too decayed to show any cause of death, supposing that violence had been used, but the general condition of the bodies does supply a strong argument. Very many of these women wear head-dresses which are delicate in themselves and would easily be disarranged, yet such are always found in good order, undisturbed except by the pressure of the earth ; this would be impossible if the wearers had been knocked on the head, improbable if they had fallen to the ground after being stabbed, and it is equally unlikely that they could have been killed outside the grave and carried down the ramp and laid in their places with all their ornaments intact ; certainly the animals must have been alive when they dragged the chariots down the ramps, and if so, the grooms who led them and the drivers in the cars must have been alive also : it is safe to assume that those who were to be sacrificed went down alive into the pit.

That they were dead, or at least unconscious, when the earth was flung in and trampled down on the top of them is an equally safe assumption, for in any other case there must have been some struggle which would have left its traces in the attitude of the bodies, but these are always decently composed ; indeed, they are in such good order and alignment that we are driven to suppose that after they were lying unconscious someone entered the pit and gave the final touches to their arrangement—and the circumstance that in A-bar-gi's grave the harps were placed on the top of the bodies proves that someone did enter the grave at the end. It is most probable that the victims walked to their places, took some kind of drug—opium or hashish would serve—and lay down in order ; after the drug had worked, whether it produced sleep or death, the last touches were given to their bodies and the pit was filled in. There does not seem to have been anything brutal in the manner of their deaths.

None the less, the sight of the remains of the victims is gruesome enough with the gold leaves and the coloured beads lying thick on the crushed and broken skulls, but in excavating a great death-pit such as that of last winter we do not see it as a whole, but have to clear it a little at a time. The soil was removed until the bodies were almost exposed, covered only by the few inches of broken brick which had been the first of the filling thrown over the dead ; here and there a pick driven too deep might bring to view a piece of gold ribbon or a golden beech leaf, showing that everywhere there were bodies richly adorned, but these would be quickly covered up again and left until more methodical work should reveal them in due course. Starting in one corner of the pit, we marked out squares such as might contain from five to six bodies, and all these were cleared, noted, and the objects belonging to them collected and removed before the next square was taken in hand.

It was slow work, and especially so in those cases where we decided to remove the entire skull with all its ornaments in position on it. The wreaths and chains and necklaces re-strung and arranged in a glass case may look very well, but it is more interesting to see them as they were actually found, and therefore a few heads on which the original order of the beads and gold-work was best preserved were laboriously cleaned with small knives and brushes, the dirt being removed without disturbing any of the ornaments—a difficult matter as they are loose in the soil—and then boiling paraffin wax was poured over them, solidifying them in one mass. The lump of wax, earth, bone, and gold was then strengthened by waxed cloth pressed carefully over it, so that it could be lifted from the ground by undercutting. Mounted in plaster, with the superfluous wax cleaned off, these heads form an exhibit which is not only of interest in itself but proves the accuracy of the restorations which we have made of others (Plate IV *a*).

Of the sixty-eight women in the pit, twenty-eight wore hair-ribbons of gold. At first sight it looked as if the others had nothing of the kind, but closer examination showed that many, if not all, had originally worn exactly similar ribbons of silver. Unfortunately silver is a metal which ill resists the action of the acids in the soil, and where it was but a thin strip and, being worn on the head, was directly affected by the corruption of the flesh, it generally disappears altogether, and at most there may be detected on the bone of the skull slight traces of a purplish colour which is silver chloride in a minutely powdered state : we could be certain that the ribbons were worn, but we could not produce material evidence of them.

But in one case we had better luck. The great gold

ear-rings were in place, but not a sign of discoloration betrayed the existence of any silver head-dress, and this negative evidence was duly noted : then, as the body was cleared, there was found against it, about on the level of the waist, a flat disk a little more than 3 inches across of a grey substance which was certainly silver ; it might have been a small circular box. Only when I was cleaning it in the house that evening, hoping to find something which would enable me to catalogue it more in detail, did its real nature come to light : it was the silver hair-ribbon, but it had never been worn—carried apparently in the woman's pocket, it was just as she had taken it from her room, done up in a tight coil with the ends brought over to prevent its coming undone ; and since it formed thus a comparatively solid mass of metal and had been protected by the cloth of her dress, it was very well preserved and even the delicate edges of the ribbon were sharply distinct. Why the owner had not put it on one could not say ; perhaps she was late for the ceremony and had not time to dress properly, but her haste has in any case afforded us the only example of a silver hair-ribbon which we are likely ever to find.

Another thing that perishes utterly in the earth is cloth, but occasionally on lifting a stone bowl which has lain inverted over a bit of stuff and has protected it from the soil one sees traces which, although only of fine dust, keep the texture of the material, or a copper vessel may by its corrosion preserve some fragment which was in contact with it. By such evidence we were able to prove that the women in the death-pit wore garments of bright red woollen stuff; and as many of them had at the wrists one or two cuffs made of beads which had been sewn on to cloth, it was tolerably certain that these were sleeved coats rather than cloaks.   It must have been a very gaily dressed crowd that assembled in the open mat-lined pit for the royal obsequies, a blaze of colour with the crimson coats, the silver, and the gold ; clearly these people were not wretched slaves killed as oxen might be killed, but persons held in honour, wearing their robes of office, and coming, one hopes, voluntarily to a rite which would in their belief be but a passing from one world to another, from the service of a god on earth to that of the same god in another sphere.

This much I think we can safely assume. Human sacrifice was confined exclusively to the funerals of royal persons, and in the graves of commoners, how-ever rich, there is no sign of anything of the sort, not even such substitutes, clay figurines, etc., as are so common in Egyptian tombs and appear there to be a reminiscence of an ancient and more bloody rite. In much later times Sumerian kings were deified in their lifetime and honoured as gods after their death : the prehistoric kings of Ur were in their obsequies so distinguished from their subjects because they too were looked upon as superhuman, earthly deities ; and when the chroniclers wrote in the annals of Sumer that ' after the Flood kingship again descended from the gods,' they meant no less than this. If the king, then, was a god, he did not die as men die, but was translated ; and it might therefore be not a hardship but a privilege for those of his court to accompany their master and continue in his service.

In the furnishing of the royal graves one constant feature is the harp or lyre ; in this great death-pit there were no less than four lyres. One of these was the most magnificent that we have yet found ; its sounding-box was bordered with a broad edging of mosaic in red and white and blue, the two uprights were encrusted with shell and lapis lazuli and red stone arranged in zones separated by wide gold bands, the cross-bar was half of plain wood, half plated with silver, shell plaques engraved with animal scenes adorned the front, and above these projected a splendid head of a bearded bull wrought in heavy gold (Plate V *a*). A second lyre was all of silver with a silver cow's head in front of the sounding-box, which was decorated with a narrow blue and white border and with shell plaques ; a third, also of silver, was in the form of a high-prowed boat on which stood a statue of a stag sculptured in the round ; the fourth, of wood but with two copper statues of stags, was almost entirely decayed, so much so that we cannot even be certain that it was a harp at all, but the first three instruments were in good condition and are amongst the finest objects found in the cemetery.

The commonest decoration of a harp or lyre is the head of an animal, and we now have the bearded bull, the cow, and, in an instrument of different form, the stag, though in this case the complete beast is shown ; the difference is not, however, so great as might appear, because in the other cases the sounding-box itself represents, though in a highly conventional, not to say 'cubist' form, the body of the animal, resolved almost entirely into straight lines, but still recognisable as such.

Now, there is an inscription by a governor Gudea (it is true that he lived a thousand years later, but tradition also is long-lived) in which he describes a

PLATE III

(a) Silver model of a boat from Tomb Pg/789.

(b)

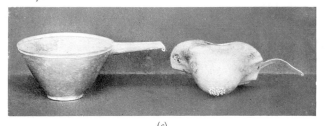

(c)

(b and c) Gold vessels of Queen Shub-ad.

PLATE IV

(a)   (b)

(a) Woman's head-dress from the Great Death-pit.
(b) The gold dagger at Ur.

harp he had presented to a temple ; it was decorated with the head of a bull, and the sound of the instrument is compared to the bellowing of the beast. If there exists such a connection between the tone of the harp and the figure represented on it, might we not assume that our instruments are of three different sorts, the bull denoting the bass, the cow the tenor, and the stag perhaps the alto ? Then the finding of four lyres together in one grave might imply a system of harmony which, at this early date, would be of very great interest for the history of music.

In a corner of the same pit there were lying two statues made of gold, lapis lazuli, and white shell ; slightly different in size, they were otherwise a pair, the subject being the same in each case. On a small oblong base decorated with silver plate and mosaic in pink and white stands a goat, ' a ram of the goats,' erect on its hind legs in front of a tree or bush to whose branches its front legs were bound with silver chains ; the leaves and flowers of the golden tree stand out high on either side, and the beast's golden head with its horns and hair of lapis lazuli peers out between them (Plate VI). Irresistibly we are reminded of the biblical story of the ' ram caught in the thicket,' but the statues were made fifteen hundred years before Abraham was born and the parallel is therefore difficult to explain. Undoubtedly the subject of the Sumerian sculpture had some religious significance ; this and similar scenes are common in the artistic repertoire of the early period and probably illustrate some well-known legend, and there is no reason to suppose that legend and illustration did not survive into a later time : the writer in Genesis may well have taken advantage of a familiar reference to point the moral of his own story ; in any case, we have here a striking anticipation of his phrase.

When the earth was thrown back into the death-pit and the tomb-chamber of the king and the bodies of the victims around it had been buried out of sight, the ritual of burial was far from being complete. Generally the upper soil of the cemetery has been so disturbed by later interments and by tomb-robbers that for a long time we failed to find any evidence of the subsequent stages of the ceremony, but in the season 1928-9 we were more fortunate.

We had been digging a patch of ground where, near the surface, the graves of commoners lay unusually thick, and were surprised to find that the shaft of one of them, containing a clay coffin, had been cut into a stout mud-brick wall. Working against the face of this, we came upon a number of clay jars, an alabaster vase, and a rectangle of faint grey lines which represented a wooden box. Scraping away the surface soil, we discovered in the box, lying side by side, two daggers of which the blades were of gold and the hilts decorated with gold studs, and between them a white shell cylinder seal inscribed with the name ' Mes-kalam-dug the King.' Next to the box was a wooden coffin containing the body of a man, but the furniture with it was by no means of the type which one would expect with a royal person, and the wall not only went further down into the soil, but as we followed it out developed into a large square of which the coffin occupied only a humble corner ; we felt sure that we had not yet found the king's grave.

Under the floor of beaten clay on which the coffin rested more clay vessels appeared forming a consistent layer over the whole area of the brick enclosure, and with these, but in another corner than that occupied by the coffin, was a second burial of a man with his weapons and vases of copper and stone. This clay floor was removed, and a fresh layer of pots and another burial came to light, and below this more layers of offerings alternating with layers of clay. Then came clean filling extending to the base of the brick walls, and at this level a

single great clay bowl put upside-down in the earth
sheltering two or three little food-bowls set out on
a piece of matting—the meal spread for the god of
the underworld.

We dug deeper down, and suddenly limestone
blocks appeared bedded in green clay and forming
a curve ; we took it to be the end of a stone vault,
and when the stones quickly dipped again feared
that the roof had been broken through by robbers ;
but another half-hour's work proved to our delight
that the masonry continued and that what we
had was a small dome absolutely intact. It was
particularly exciting because the top of the dome
had been built over a centring supported by stout
beams which ran right through the stone-work, and
the decay of these had left half a dozen holes in the
roof through which one could glimpse parts of the
dim interior and by the light of electric torches
could even see on the floor below the shapes of
green copper vessels and catch an occasional glint
of gold.

We cleared down to the level of the tops of the
walls of the tomb-chamber, and at each corner,
resting on the heavy clay which filled the space
between the walls and the sides of the pit, found
the ashes of fires and broken clay pots and animal

bones. In front of the chamber door were laid the
carcases of three sheep. The stone blocking of the
door was pulled away, and inside, beneath the
remains of rotten wood fallen from the ceiling, lay
five bodies ; four of them were those of men—
servants, judging from their poor equipment, and
the fifth was that of a woman ; she had the golden
head-dress of one of high rank, a long curved golden
pin such as we had not seen before fastened her
cloak, in her hands was a fluted and engraved
tumbler of gold, and by her side a golden cylinder
seal, the first we have ever found : this clearly was
the queen.

Now the ritual of the interment could be under-
stood. The royal body with its attendants, many or
few, was laid in the tomb, and the door was sealed
and sacrifice was made in the little court before the
entrance, and then this was filled in until only the
crown of the dome was left above ground. Round
it fires were lit and a funeral feast was held, and
libations to the dead were poured into a clay drain
which ran down into the soil beside the tomb, and
then more earth was thrown into the shaft. Next
an offering to the under-gods was set out and
covered with a clay bowl to shield it from the fresh
earth which buried it ; and then, in the half-filled

pit, there was constructed in mud brick what was
to be a subterranean building.

The filling-up of this building was done by degrees;
clay was brought and trampled hard to make a floor
over which offerings were spread and on which was
laid the body of a human victim sacrificed in these
later rites ; earth buried these, and another floor
was made and more offerings placed in order and
another victim did honour to the dead below, and
this went on till the top of the walls was nearly
reached ; then half of the building was roofed in
with a vault of mud brick, and in this subsidiary
tomb was put the coffin of one whom we may suppose to have been the chief sacrifice, and here king
Mes-kalam-dug dedicated to the un-named queen
his golden daggers and the seal bearing his title.
Then this chamber too was buried under the filling
of the shaft, and probably on the top of it all there
was erected on the ground-surface some kind of
funerary chapel which should perpetuate the
sanctity of the spot.

Each stage of this elaborate procedure must have
been marked by some religious service, and the
whole ceremony must have taken a long time ; the
details of it very likely varied in different cases, but
the discovery of a second royal tomb (unfortunately

plundered) with layers of offerings above it exactly corresponding to that just described proves that this is no isolated case but illustrates the normal ritual for the burial of a king.

As I have said above, there was no such ritual for the commoner. Last winter we found the grave of a ' court lady ' wearing the golden head-dress familiar to us from the royal tombs, and amongst the offerings set alongside her coffin there was even a harp, a simpler edition of the type found with queen Shub-ad ; but here there were no victims sacrificed in her honour, and we can only suppose that she was a private person and that the harp was her personal property which she wished to take with her to another world, just as someone else might take a gaming-board or a toilet-box.

The body of a little girl not more than six or seven years old was adorned with a head-dress almost as elaborate as queen Shub-ad's own, but on a minia-ture scale, tiny gold rings across the forehead, tiny gold beech leaves hanging from the strings of lapis and carnelian beads ; she grasped a gold cup only about 2 inches high, and by her side were two silver bowls and a fluted tumbler reproducing in miniature those from the queen's tomb ; our workmen called this ' the grave of the little princess,' but she lay in it alone and could boast none of the blood-offerings of kings. But the best proof of the gulf that separated king from commoner was given by the grave of Mes-kalam-dug discóvered in the season 1927–8, a grave dug down into the shaft of the largest of all the stone-built royal tombs.

The first indication we had of what was to come was a copper spear-head sticking straight up in the ground ; following this down we found that it was attached to a golden haft, and below this was the hole left by the decay of the wooden shaft running down to a corner of the grave. Except for the fact that it was rather larger than usual, the grave was a normal one, a plain earth pit big enough to take a wooden coffin and to leave on three sides of this a free space for offerings. Along the head of the grave were stuck spears in a row, the blades downwards, and between these were vases of alabaster and clay ; by the side of the coffin, lying on the remains of what may have been a bossed shield, were two gold-mounted daggers, copper daggers, chisels and other tools, some fifty copper bowls, many of them fluted, and other bowls of silver, copper jugs and plates, and more vessels of stone and clay ; at the foot of the grave again spears, and with them a set of arrows having chisel-edged points of chipped flint.

But it was when the earth from the coffin itself was removed that we had our great surprise—and as the discovery was made soon after our disappointment with the first of the stone-built royal graves, when only the golden dagger of the year before had given us an inkling of what treasures the cemetery might yield, our surprise was the greater. The body lay in normal fashion on its right side ; round the waist was a broad belt of silver, now decayed, from which hung a gold dagger and a whetstone of lapis lazuli fixed on a gold ring ; in front of the waist was a solid mass of lapis and gold beads, hundreds in all ; between the hands was placed a bowl of heavy gold, a larger oval gold bowl lay close by, and near the elbow a gold lamp in the form of a shell, while yet another gold bowl stood behind the head. Against the right shoulder was a double axe-head of electrum, and an electrum axe-head of normal type was by the left shoulder ; behind the body there were jumbled together in a heap a gold head-dress, bracelets, beads, and amulets, lunate ear-rings, and spiral rings of gold wire.

The bones were so far decayed that there was here none of the grimness of a skeleton, only a few strips of crumbling brown which served to show the attitude of the dead man, and the prevailing note was struck rather by the gold, clean as when it was put into the grave ; and most of all was the eye taken by the helmet which still covered the rotten fragments of the skull. It was a helmet of beaten gold made to fit low over the head with cheek-pieces to protect the face, and it was in the form of a wig, the locks of hair hammered up in relief, the individual hairs shown by delicate engraved lines. Parted down the middle the hair covers the head in flat wavy tresses and is bound round with a twisted fillet ; behind it is tied into a little chignon, and below the fillet hangs in rows of formal curls about the ears, which are rendered in high relief and are pierced so as not to interfere with hearing ; similar curls on the cheek-pieces represent whiskers ; round the edge of the metal are small holes for the laces which secured inside it a padded cap, of which some traces yet remained.

As an example of goldsmith's work this is the most beautiful thing we have found in the cemetery, finer than the gold daggers or the heads of bulls, and if there were nothing else by which the art of these ancient Sumerians could be judged we should still, on the strength of it alone, accord them high rank in the roll of civilised races.

On two of the golden bowls and on the lamp was

repeated the inscription ' Mes-kalam-dug, Hero of the Good Land.' The name is the same as that found on the cylinder seal dedicated with the two gold daggers above the domed stone tomb of a queen, but the owner of the seal is called ' King,' and here there is no such title of royalty : the term ' Hero of the Good Land ' and the exceptional richness of the grave may justify us in seeing in this Mes-kalam-dug a prince of the royal house, but the omission of any claim to kingly power ought certainly to mean that he never occupied the throne, and this omission is precisely what we should expect if our theory is correct, for the grave is essentially of the commoner's type and contains no subsidiary burials, no hint of human sacrifice. Had the royal tombs not been discovered, this would probably have been hailed as a king's grave ; as it is, its wealth only emphasises the difference between it and them.

While trying to give some idea of what the graves are like and describing some of the treasures they contain, I have said very little about the condition of the objects at the time of finding. It is true that no imagination was required to grasp the splendour of Mes-kalam-dug's grave, because the objects in that were for the most part of gold, and gold is imperishable ; a gold bowl may be crushed or dinted, but its colour and its surface remain and every detail of its workmanship and decoration is as clear as when it was newly wrought ; but other materials are less enduring—I have spoken of the way in which silver corrodes and even vanishes— and suffer both from internal decay and from the crushing weight of the 30 or 40 feet of earth below which they have lain buried for five thousand years. Often it is difficult to remove from the soil without further damage an object which it is essential to preserve ; sometimes it is hard even to judge of the object's nature and importance ; nearly always some measure of repair or restoration is required before the thing is fit for exhibition, and the restoration may be the most laborious task of all.

As an illustration of this I would take one of the two statues of rams found in the great death-pit. The figure was made as follows. The head and legs were carved in wood, the horns of lapis and the inlaid eyes being fixed in position by copper rivets driven through the head, and then gold, little thicker than gold leaf, was laid over them, a thin wash of bitumen acting as glue to fix the metal on to the wood. The head and legs were mortised into a rudimentary wooden body which was next rounded off into proper shape with plaster of paris and given a thick coat of bitumen ; a thin silver plate was fixed over the belly, and into the bitumen covering back and sides were pressed the locks of hair, each carved separately from a piece of white shell or, for the shoulders, in lapis lazuli ; the tree was also of wood overlaid with gold leaf, the leaves and flowers made of double gold and fixed on after the trunk and branches were complete.

When we found them, both statues were in very sorry plight. The wood had decayed to nothing, the bitumen was dry powder, the plaster of paris reduced to irregular lumps and pellets ; one figure was lying on its side, crushed absolutely flat so that the shell curls of the two flanks touched each other and the animal was a mere silhouette distorted by pressure, the other, standing upright, preserved some of its roundness but had been telescoped together and the legs had been broken off from the body, flattened and twisted. Nothing except the earth around them kept the fragments of lapis and shell inlay in position, and if that position were once lost, there would have been no guide at all for the restoration of the figure ; the whole thing was therefore solidified with hot wax poured liberally on, and then bands of waxed muslin were applied to every exposed part until the ram was as securely wrapped up as a mummy and could be lifted from the earth.

For restoration, the waxed wrappings were softened with heat sufficiently for the sides of the beast to be pressed apart and the dirt removed from inside its body ; then wax and bandages were applied to the interior, the outer bandages removed, and with gentle heating the body could be pushed out into its original shape, and that without dislodging the inlaid locks of the fleece now adhering to the inner coating of wax. The complete decay of the silver over the belly really facilitated the task, because it gave a chance to work at the body from the inside through a comparatively large opening. The legs were straightened, and with slender tools inserted down the tubes of them the dinted gold was pressed out again as much as possible, then copper wires were put down them and a boiling mixture of wax and bitumen poured in to make all solid. The head presented greater difficulties, because the thin gold leaf was broken into eighteen small fragments and these were badly crushed and bent ; each had to be unfolded, worked out to its original curve and strengthened from the back, and then the joints had to be found and the different morsels brought together and fixed with due regard to the curves of their outer face. It was a jigsaw puzzle in three dimensions, but in time the head took shape and character. Plastic wood was used to fill the body and to secure the wires of the legs, the belly was painted with silver paint to replace the perished metal, and the statue was complete (Plate VI).

Of course, methods of this kind cannot reproduce all the *finesse* of the original ; to do that one would have to take the whole thing to pieces and re-create ; but in so doing one loses something which is of sentimental if not always of scientific importance— the object as exhibited is really a copy, new throughout, of the old work, and no one can be quite certain of its faithfulness. In dealing with the antiquities from Ur we have preferred a restoration which implies the least possible interference with the object to a reconstruction which may give a better appearance but depends more on the modern hand.

Another instance will make the point clearer. In the largest of all the stone-built royal tombs, which had been entered by robbers and most thoroughly plundered, there remained only one corner of the last chamber to be cleared, and we had given up expectation of any ' finds ' when suddenly a loose bit of shell inlay turned up, and the next minute the foreman's hand, carefully brushing away the earth, laid bare the corner of a mosaic in lapis lazuli and shell. This was the famous ' Standard ' of Ur, but at the time we had very little idea of what it might be : the wooden background had perished entirely, and the tiny pieces of inlay, though they kept their relative positions in the soil, were all quite loose ; falling stones had bent and twisted the once flat panel, while as the wood decayed and the fragments sank back into the empty space behind, their different thickness made the surface of them rough and uneven. So delicate was the task of removing the dirt without further disturbing the mosaic that only about a square inch could be dealt with at a time—each section was waxed as soon as cleared, but so much of the surrounding dirt mingled with the hot wax that the face of the panel became invisible. When at last it could be lifted from the earth, I knew that we had found a very fine thing, but should have been hard put to it to say exactly what it was.

Now, it would have been perfectly feasible to take the mosaic to pieces, bit by bit, and re-make it on a new background, and the task might have been done as well by the modern craftsman as by the old, but the panels would have been the work of a modern craftsman.

PLATE V

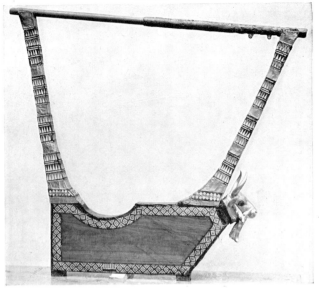

(*a*) Gold and mosaic harp from the Great Death-pit.

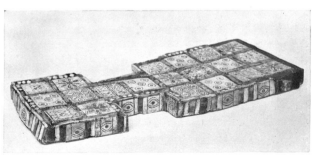

(*b*) An inlaid gaming-board.

PLATE VI

The statue of ' a ram caught in a thicket.'

What was done was this. The two sides of the panel were separated, and waxed cloth was fixed to the back of the inlay and the face of it was roughly cleaned ; it was then laid face downwards on glass and warmed until the wax was soft, and it was pressed with the fingers from behind until by looking underneath one could be sure that each fragment of the inlay was in direct contact with the glass. The panel was now flat, but the pattern was much distorted ; the edges of the mosaic fragments had lost contact in the ground and earth and powdered bitumen had filtered between them, and now wax as well, so that while some overlapped, others were widely apart. The next stage was to remove the cloth from the back, leaving the mosaic virtually loose on the glass, and to pick out all foreign matter, and then by sideways pressure with the fingers coax the pieces together. When this was done, fresh wax and cloth were applied behind and a proper backing fixed on.

The result of this is that the mosaic is not nearly so regular or smooth as the Sumerian artist made it, but what we possess is the work of that artist uninterfered with except by the accidents of time ; the pieces of shell and lapis which he put together no one else has taken apart and re-set (Plate VII).

F

In the case of the ' Standard ' the labour of restoration was at the same time a process of discovery ; the work in the field had really been done in the dark, and it was only when the panels were cleaned and had begun to take shape in the laboratory that their importance could be recognised. There are two main panels, rectangular and measuring 22 inches long by 9 inches high, and two triangular pieces which formed the ends ; these were fixed together so that the larger sides sloped inwards and the whole thing was fastened on to the end of a pole, and would seem to have been carried in processions ; we actually found it lying against the shoulder of a man who may have been the king's standard-bearer.

The mosaic is composed of figures silhouetted in shell with details engraved which are set in a background of lapis lazuli, relieved here and there with red. The triangular ends have mythological scenes of animals ; the main panels illustrate respectively Peace and War. On one side the king and the royal family are seen at feast. They sit in chairs, their costume consists of the old-fashioned sheep-skin kilt or petticoat and the upper part of the body is bare ; servants wait on them, and at one end of the scene is a musician playing on a small harp, while by him a woman singer with her hands to her breast sings to the accompaniment of the instrument.

These figures form the top row of the design ; in two lower rows attendants are shown bringing in spoils captured from the enemy and food-supplies for the banquet—one is driving a goat, another carries two fish, another is bent under the weight of a corded bale, and so on, several of the figures being repeated. On the other side, in the centre of the top row, stands the king, distinguished by his greater height, with behind him three attendants or members of his house, and a dwarf-like groom who holds the heads of the two asses which draw the monarch's empty chariot while the driver of it walks behind holding the reins ; in front of the king soldiers are bringing up prisoners, naked and with their arms bound behind their backs, for him to decide their fate.

In the second row, at the back, comes the phalanx of the royal army, heavy-armed infantry in close order with copper helmets exactly like those found by us in the king's grave, and long cloaks of some stiff material which I take to be felt, just such cloaks as are worn by the shepherds of Anatolia to-day, holding axes in their hands ; in front of them are the light-armed infantry without cloaks, wielding axes or short spears, already engaged with an enemy whose naked warriors are either fleeing or being struck down.

In the lowest row we have the chariotry of Sumer, each car drawn by two asses and carrying two men, of whom one is the driver and the other a warrior who flings light javelins, of which four are kept in a quiver tied to the front of the car. The chariots advance over the battlefield, and by a naturalistic touch the artist of the ' Standard ' makes the asses at the rear walk sedately, while those drawing the other cars become more and more excited as they encounter the corpses strewn on the ground, until those in front have broken into a gallop which threatens the balance of the riders.

The ' Standard ' is a remarkable work of art, but it has yet greater value as an historical document, for here we have figured the earliest detailed picture of that army which carried the civilisation of the Sumerians from their early settlements on the fringe of the Persian Gulf to the mountains of Anatolia and to the shores of the Mediterranean Sea. We know from actual examples found in their graves that their weapons were, both in design and in manufacture, far superior to anything that their contemporaries possessed or any other nation was to adopt for two

thousand years ; from this representation we can
learn enough about the organisation of the army
to know that it must have been more than a match
for anything that could be brought against it at that
time. The chariotry which was to inspire an almost
superstitious terror in the Hebrews of the time of
the Judges had been used by the Sumerians more
than two thousand years before, and the phalanx
which won Alexander his victories had been antici-
pated by them : it is not surprising that until they
had taught their neighbours to profit by their
example they found no opponent to withstand their
advance.

This is the story of the excavations at Ur, not a
history of the Sumerian people, but something must
be said here to show how important those excavations have been for our knowledge of early civilisation. The contents of the tombs illustrate a very
highly developed state of society of an urban type,
a society in which the architect was familiar with
all the basic principles of construction known to us
to-day. The artist, capable at times of a most vivid
realism, followed for the most part standards and
conventions whose excellence had been approved
by many generations working before him ; the
craftsman in metal possessed a knowledge of

metallurgy and a technical skill which few ancient
peoples ever rivalled ; the merchant carried on a
far-flung trade and recorded his transactions in
writing ; the army was well organised and victor-
ious, agriculture prospered, and great wealth gave
scope to luxury. Our tombs date, as has already
been said, between 3500 and 3200 B.C., and as the
nature of the civilisation would lead one to expect,
and as has been demonstrated by the discoveries in
the rubbish below the tombs described in the last
chapter, by 3500 B.C. this civilisation was already
many centuries old.

Until recently it was thought that the Egyptian
civilisation was the oldest in the world and that it
was the fountain-head wherefrom the later civilisa-
tions of other Western countries drew at any rate
the inspiration which informed them. But in
3500 B.C. Egypt was still barbarous, divided into
petty kingdoms not yet united by ' Menes,' the
founder of the First Dynasty, into a single state.
When Egypt does make a start, the beginnings of a
new age are marked by the introduction of models
and ideas which derive from that older civilisation
which, as we know now, had long been developing
and flourishing in the Euphrates valley, and to the
Sumerians we can trace much that is at the root not

only of Egyptian, but also of Babylonian, Assyrian, Hebrew, and Phœnician art and thought, and so see that the Greeks also were in debt to this ancient and for long forgotten people, the pioneers of the progress of Western man. It is this that makes excavation in the oldest levels at Ur of such absorbing interest, the knowledge that almost every object found is not merely an illustration of the achievement of a particular race at a particular time, but also a new document helping to fill up the picture of those beginnings from which is derived our modern world.

Chapter III

Al 'Ubaid and the Earliest Written History

IN 1919 DR. H. R. HALL, WORKING FOR THE BRITISH Museum, found, in what might be called a suburb of Ur, a little mound some four miles from the centre of the city, ruins of very early date and very remarkable character. He traced round three sides the outer face of a rectangular building constructed with the small round-topped bricks called ' plano-convex ' which are only used in the earliest times, and against one face came upon a hoard of objects lying tumbled together under a mass of mud brick.

There was a small stone statue of a man carved in the primitive and summary style already familiar to us from stray examples procured elsewhere, but with this were other monuments of a more novel sort. There was a great copper relief 7 ft. 9 ins. long and 3 ft. 6 ins. high, representing in heraldic fashion an eagle grasping two stags ; there were the fore parts of lions, nearly life-size, made of copper hammered over bitumen and wood with inlaid eyes and white shell teeth through which protruded tongues of red stone ; there were fragments of wooden columns incrusted with mother-of-pearl, red stone, and black shale ; clay flowers with inlaid petals of white, black, and red, and more heads of animals in copper but on a smaller scale. Altogether it was a most important discovery, and since the excavation was left unfinished by Dr. Hall, it was the obvious duty of the Joint Expedition to complete it as soon as possible. In the season 1923–4, therefore, a branch camp was set up at al 'Ubaid (such is the name of the little mound), and the work was restarted with the hope that more light would be thrown on the nature of the building and that there might yet be objects awaiting discovery.

Dr. Hall's work had given us a warning. The copper statues found by him had suffered terribly through corrosion and breakage, and, important as they were, were but ghosts of the originals ; of the lions' heads little more remained than the bitumen cores with the inlay of eyes and mouth, of the columns only the loose fragments of the incrustation could be collected and brought home, and the great copper relief, of which only one stag's head was recovered intact, had to be reconstructed from fragments, and in several respects the reconstruction was open to doubt. If, then, we should encounter any further objects of the kind we had to be sure that our resources would be adequate to the delicate task of their removal and transport.

The work of excavation which had produced the original hoard of statuary had begun at one corner of the building and had been carried on not quite to its central point when the diggers had encountered and partly cut into a particularly solid mass of mud brick. We started at this point and, following up the brickwork—with some difficulty, for it showed no true face—found that it was one side of a staircase projecting at right angles from the main building; the treads, of which a number were preserved at the stairs' foot, were great slabs of white limestone, the first example of the use of stone for building that had been noted in the south of Mesopotamia except for a similar flight of stairs leading up to the staged tower of Abu Shahrein, a ruin about 12 miles south of Ur. Further examination proved that the building itself was a solid mass of brick, a platform approached by the flight of steps, and only the substructure of a building which itself had completely disappeared.

Working round the stairway and following the wall between it and the far corner of the platform we found, under a mass of mud brick of a later period (a new platform laid down over the ruins of the old), a second hoard of objects in part similar to those which had rewarded Dr. Hall and in part different. In the angle between the stairs and the wall there lay two ten-foot columns of wood encrusted with mother-of-pearl, shale, and red stone, and other palm-log columns and beams overlaid with sheets of copper ; piled in one heap there were four copper statues of bulls standing upright with their heads turned outwards over their shoulders ; in a line along the wall were copper reliefs of reclining cattle, and mixed with these sections of mosaic friezes in which figures silhouetted in white limestone or in shell were set against a background of black shale and framed with strips of copper ; and everywhere in the soil we found fragments or complete examples of the inlaid clay flowers with cone-like stems which had figured in the earlier excavations.

One day a workman unearthed before my eyes a small oblong tablet of white limestone bearing an inscription ; I handed it to Mr. Gadd, who was standing beside me, and he read it out : ' A-anni-pad-da King of Ur, son of Mes-anni-pad-da King of Ur, has built this for his Lady Nin-kharsag.' It was the foundation-stone of the building, and the most important of all our discoveries.

At first reading it does not sound a very exciting thing, a list of rather unpronounceable names, but we were excited enough. The first name was unknown to us or anyone, but the second was familiar, and not only proved the date of the building but cleared up a whole chapter in ancient history.

There exist copies, dating back before 2000 B.C., of lists drawn up by Sumerian scribes of the kings who, according to their successive dynasties, ruled the lower valley of the Two Rivers. The later dynasties were known to be historical, because independent monuments of their kings had been found, but the earlier dynasties had been rejected by modern students as mythical, partly because nothing was known about them, mainly because the scribes who composed the lists attributed to the early rulers a longevity which outdoes Methuselah. The third dynasty after the Flood is in the lists assigned to the kings of Ur and is called the First Dynasty of Ur, and its founder, who is given a reign of eighty years, is Mes-anni-pad-da and is succeeded by Meskiag-Nannar.

Now we had in our hands a contemporary written document which proved the existence of the founder of the First Dynasty of Ur and established the historical truth of the ancient king-lists, while at the same time it cleared up the only difficulty which they presented. Mes-anni-pad-da had a son who does not appear in the lists, but who actually suc-

ceeded his father on the throne, and the names of
the two were so much alike that a not unnatural
confusion resulted, and the reigns of the two were
lumped together and their total span of eighty years
attributed to the better-known founder of the royal
house ; divide that figure by inserting A-anni-pad-
da's reign, and the only improbability disappears.
But our tablet not only proved the accuracy of the
written lists ; it gave to our building a more or less
accurate date, about 3100 B.C., so that the objects
belonging to it could be considered in their proper
place in the sequence of the development of art ;
and it meant that the First Dynasty of Ur was no
longer just a list of names, but stood for a period in
history whose character and achievements we now
have material to judge ; a whole age was resuscitated
and made real by that one small stone.

But the objects to which so much extra interest was
lent by the finding of the foundation-tablet gave us a
very anxious time ; they lay so thickly in the ground
that there might be half a dozen of them all exposed
at one time and all calling for special care in their
removal ; and their condition was quite as bad as
we had feared.

The uppermost of the four copper bulls was barely
recognisable, only part of one leg and a mass of

green powder betraying its existence. The second looked more promising, but the metal was broken into a thousand pieces and was so soft that it crumbled to dust at a touch (I spent three weeks preparing it and then when we lifted it the whole thing collapsed in atoms) ; with the next two we had better success and they are now in the British Museum and at Philadelphia, battered and distorted figures but still figures of bulls showing something of the fine quality of the originals and remarkable as being the oldest copper statues preserved to us. The copper reliefs were less difficult to manage and only one was rejected as too fragmentary for removal, and even then the head, cast in metal and more solid than the hammered sheets which formed the body, remained a first-class object.

The inlaid columns were crushed flat and the wood had perished, but most of the tesseræ were approximately in position, only those along the edges having been dislodged and scattered. They were removed in sections, sacking being waxed on to the tesseræ that lay face upwards and glued on to the backs of those which belonged to the lower face of the shafts ; lifted thus in sheets, the decoration could be fixed on to a new core (it was found that circular petrol-drums were of exactly the right diameter, and these served

our turn) without any disturbance of the individual
bits of stone and mother-of-pearl, while other sheets
and the loose tesseræ collected from the earth were
kept with a view to more drastic reconstruction.

The mosaic friezes were held together with wax
and muslin for such treatment as the Museum
authorities might choose to give them. The friezes
were two in number. One was simple, a row of
birds, probably doves, rather roughly cut in white
limestone (which I think was originally painted in
colour) against a black ground. The other was much
more elaborate and showed much finer workmanship. It consisted for most of its length of a procession of cows carved in limestone, probably once
painted, or in shell, which was probably left white,
but in the centre there was a scene in which human
figures are introduced ; on one side of a reed-built
byre, from the door of which two calves are seen
issuing, men seated on low stools are milking cattle ;
the man sits under the cow's tail milking her from
behind ; the calves, duly muzzled, are roped to the
cows' head-stalls so as to encourage them to give
milk. On the other side of the byre two men,
clean-shaven and wearing the fleece petticoat which
in later times seems to survive as the official dress
of priests and priest-kings, are pouring milk through

a strainer into a vessel set on the ground, while two others are collecting the strained liquid in great store-jars (Plate VIII *a*).

It is a typical scene of pastoral life, but the costume of the actors makes it likely that it is something more than this. There were in later days at least sacred farms attached to the temples, and here we may have priests preparing the milk of the Mother-goddess Nin-kharsag which was the nourishment of kings. That the very domestic-looking picture of milking had a religious bearing is made more likely by the fact that in the same frieze there was introduced between the figures of walking cattle a small panel of a curiously incongruous character : it shows a bearded bull rampant in hilly country, on whose back is perched a lion-headed eagle apparently attacking him and tearing at his rump ; this is certainly an illustration of some mythological legend and its presence here cannot but affect our view of the frieze as a whole.

All the objects found were clearly elements in the architectural decoration of the building and would gain enormously in interest if they could be assigned to their proper places in the scheme. This was not easy, because of the building itself there was not a single brick left in position, and of the platform

PLATE VII

The mosaic 'Standard' of Ur.

PLATE VIII

(*a*) Mosaic frieze from the temple at al 'Ubaid.

(*b*) The temple at al 'Ubaid restored.

which supported it the upper part had been destroyed, so that even the ground-plan was unknown. Fortunately, it proved possible, by taking the exact position of every object in its relation to the wall and the exact angle at which it lay, and by calculating the slope of the layers of debris against the wall-face and the height of the objects in that debris, to get a very fairly accurate idea of the position from which each had fallen or, where things had been thrown out, of the place from which the people who violently destroyed the temple must have thrown them, and so to work out the original plan and character of the building (Plate VIII *b*).

The temple proper occupied one corner of the platform and its main door stood at the top of the flight of stone steps ; it stood a little back from the platform's edge, and in front of its door there was a porch with a pent-house roof whose beams and supporting columns were of wood overlaid with polished copper. Mosaic columns held up the lintel, and above this was set into the wall the copper relief of the eagle and two stags found by Dr. Hall, while the front parts of lions found by him had their place in re-entrant angles flanking the actual doorway, which they thus seemed to guard.

On the ledge along the top of the platform, against

G

the background of the temple wall, stood the copper
statues of bulls, and round them, probably, were
set the clay flowers standing upright so as to give
the effect of animals in a flowery meadow. Higher
up on the façade came the copper frieze of reclining
cattle worked in relief; above these the mosaic
frieze with the milking-scene; and higher up still
the bird frieze with its bolder and more roughly-
carved figures. The brick balustrades of the staircase were certainly panelled with wood, for we found
along the foot of them the copper nails by which the
wood was attached; the platform was of burnt
brick below, and this may well have been left exposed; the upper part, of mud brick, was probably
whitewashed, as was the mud-brick wall of the
temple above.

We can picture the whole building as something
very gay and fanciful, the gold and colour of its
decoration vivid against the white walls, and we
can admire the skill with which the elements of the
decoration are graded according to their height from
the ground—statues in the round below, then figures
in relief, then flat figures seen as silhouettes against
the black bands of the friezes—and the knowledge of
perspective which prefers simpler and broader
effects for the top row of all. We shall admire the

more if we recognise that it is the oldest building in Mesopotamia and one of the earliest in the world which we can re-create more or less as it really was.

In a second and smaller mound which lay close to the temple we found a number of graves. Compared to those of the early cemetery at Ur they were very poor, containing as they did few objects other than pottery, but they were, in spite of that, most important. It was natural to suppose that they should be contemporary with A-anni-pad-da's building, since the neighbourhood of a temple is holy ground and is therefore generally a favourite spot for burying the dead ; but besides this, some of the clay vessels of very distinctive form found in the graves were actually represented in the milking-scene on the mosaic frieze ; the graves could be confidently assigned to the First Dynasty of Ur, and since they supplied us with a great variety of pottery types used in that period, we had an admirable starting-point for dating subsequent discoveries.

In all excavations, whether in building sites or in graveyards, pottery forms the bulk of the objects found. In every country the forms of clay vessels in common use change from age to age as civilisation advances or degenerates, new social conditions have to be met, new inventions are introduced or simply

fashions alter : a few types may be fairly constant
throughout a long period, but on the whole pots
change with the times, and while the same is true
of all other things, pots, as being the most numerous
and, since baked clay is for all its fragility virtually
indestructible, the best preserved, are the most
useful evidence for dating. In a country like Egypt,
where the domestic pottery of every age has been
carefully studied and recorded, it is possible to fix
the age of a ruin by merely walking over the mounds
and observing the sherds which strew the surface ;
in Mesopotamia in 1923 very little was known of the
pottery of any period and that of the early times was
absolutely unknown. To secure more than a hundred shapes of vases and to learn the kind of ware
employed in making them, with the certainty that
all belonged to a definite period in history, was most
valuable, and when we came to excavate the rich
tombs of Ur it was partly on the basis of the graves
of al 'Ubaid that we were able to assign to them
their true date.

The First Dynasty of Ur, which with the discoveries just described emerged from the mists of
legend into the world of reality, is poorly represented by buildings in the city of Ur itself, at least
so far as our excavations have gone as yet. A few

broken walls of ' plano-convex ' brick, in one case built like the platform of al 'Ubaid on foundations of limestone blocks, are all that have survived the ravages of time and the constant demolition and rebuilding of old sites by men, but a certain number of objects have come to light which belong to that age.

In the cemetery two or three graves have been found which seem to be later than the rest and may overlap into the time of the First Dynasty, and probably there were more which have been plundered and destroyed ; this would account for a discovery made at no great depth from the modern surface, the discovery of a lapis lazuli cylinder seal, lying loose in the soil and coming from some ruined grave, on which was inscribed the name of the wife of king Mes-anni-pad-da, the mother, as we may suppose, of him who built the temple at al 'Ubaid ; two generations of the royal house are now represented by contemporary inscriptions. On grounds of style we may assign to the same date a stone fragment found close to a First Dynasty brick floor buried in the rubbish on the south-west outskirts of the cemetery ; it is the lower half of a limestone slab on which is carved in relief a scene of the funeral procession of a king ; the empty chariot, covered with a spotted leopard's skin, drawn

by two beasts which look like lions but ought by
analogy to be asses (their heads are broken away),
is led along by attendants ; there was another scene
above which is lost.

Under the foundations of a house attached to one
of the temples another discovery was made. The
ground here had been terraced for the building,
and tumbled together in the filling behind the
terrace wall was a group of objects of First Dynasty
date. Two of these were a pair, limestone figures of
rams, only the heads and foreparts carved in the
round, the rest left rough ; they seem to be supports for a throne, probably the seat of some statue
of a god whose sacred emblem was the ram. With
them was a small relief in alabaster carved on both
sides ; it was badly weathered and only half of it
was preserved, but it was curiously interesting. It
represented a high-prowed boat made of reeds tied
together and having an arched cabin or canopy
amidships—a boat not unlike the silver model found
in the tomb of the king A-bar-gi ; on one side a man
was shown standing in the stern and a sow in the
cabin, on the other two fish took the place of the man
and a goose that of the sow. Probably the little
object was dedicated in a temple by one of the marsh
folk and pictures the sort of life he led, for fish, wild

geese, and wild boar are the staple products of the marsh-land ; it was a strong temptation to call it a picture of Noah's Ark ! but though that passed as a jest in camp, the other is the more likely explanation !

The First Dynasty, when Ur was the capital of all the South Country, must have been a very rich and prosperous time, and at any moment we may light upon some important work of its kings hidden under the mounds of the city ; but even without that we have, thanks to al 'Ubaid, a remarkable illustration of their achievements. The dynasty came to a violent end and the sovereignty of Sumer passed to other hands and to another city, and the long period of subjection which followed is unmarked by any monuments. The work which we have done round the Ziggurat has afforded proof that already in the First Dynasty there was a great staged tower attached to the temple of the Moon-god, which is indeed no more than we should expect, and some remains of mud-brick walls there give evidence of repairs or rebuilding carried out perhaps in the time of a short-lived Second Dynasty of kings of whom even the names are unknown.

It was while we were clearing the back of the Ziggurat that we came upon something which tells not of the glories of Ur but of its humiliation. Fallen to the ground and lying on a brick pavement of very late date there was a large diorite statue of a man wearing the sheep-skin petticoat and bearing engraved on his back and shoulders a long inscription giving his name, Entemena, king of Lagash, one of the cities which for a time held the hegemony of the valley and accounted themselves suzerains of Ur. The head was missing ; it had been broken off deliberately in antiquity, and the jagged stump of the neck was polished as if by the con-temptuous caresses of innumerable hands, and it is natural to suppose that the statue, set up by the overlord in his vassal city, had been mutilated and dishonoured by the inhabitants when for a space they regained their lost independence.

Entemena lived about 2750 B.C. and it is to this period that we may assign another object found preserved in the treasury of the temple of the Moon-goddess. This is a limestone slab carved in relief and perfectly preserved. There are two scenes upon it ; in the upper a figure which, judging from its greater size, is probably that of the king, followed by the smaller figures of his sons, is pouring a libation in front of the statue of a seated god ; in the lower the door of a shrine is represented, and in front of it a naked priest is making his libation, while behind him stands a woman in long garments and two attendants bearing offerings for the sacrifice. The scene is one of a series whose historical importance I shall describe later.

Of all the rulers who made themselves masters of Lower Mesopotamia in these troubled times of warring city-states the most famous was Sargon, a Semite who rebelled against his master and founded a new city of Agade or Akkad, which was to give its name to the whole North Country, so that ' King of Sumer and Akkad ' became the regular title of the suzerain lord. For a long time it was supposed that he had no real historical existence, that under this fictitious name were grouped the deeds or the legends of a number of forgotten kings, and he was identified, perhaps rightly, with the Nimrod of the Old Testament who founded Caleh and was a mighty hunter before the Lord. Later documents were found which established the fact of his life and power, and now at Ur we have relics which add something to his history and illustrate the civilisation of his time.

Above the early cemetery of the prehistoric kings of Ur lie other graves, quite distinct from them, and distinguished by the difference of their contents.

These belong to the time of Sargon of Akkad.
The graves themselves are just like those of the
early period, but the forms of the pottery are all new,
and from the fact that much more care has been
spent on their manufacture and that attention is
paid to the appearance of the vessel, which might
be covered with a wash of red paint and then
brightly burnished, it may perhaps be argued that
wealth was less than of old, for it is when men
cannot afford cups and dishes of stone or metal that
the humbler art of the potter comes into its own.
Weapons, too, are very different ; instead of the
beautifully designed and admirably cast socketed
axes of the older period, a clumsily shaped blade is
simply hammered round the end of the wooden haft
and made fast by a rivet ; similarly the socketed
arrow-head disappears, and is replaced by one with
a tang which was driven into the shaft ; everywhere
there is less grace and inferior technique.

Fashions change in other things too ; the old elaborate head-dress of the women with wreaths of gold
leaves and gold hair-ribbons, and the man's head-
band of gold chains and big beads of lapis lazuli and
gold which kept the head-cloth in place, are found
no longer ; instead, an oval plate of the thinnest gold
is tied across the forehead and two slender ribbons

of gold are twisted spirally round two locks of hair which are brought from each side round over the brow and pinned one above the other.

We did find last winter one grave of this Sargonid age the riches of which recalled the great days of queen Shub-ad. It was a man's grave, and he wore not one but six of the oval gold frontlets on his head, heavy gold bracelets on his arms, gold finger-rings, quantities of beads, and with these had a gold amulet in the form of a standing goat very finely cast, and two lapis lazuli cylinder seals mounted in gold ; he also wore a single gold ear-ring, which seems to have been the male fashion, since single ear-rings often occur in men's graves. But this was an exceptional case, so much so that it emphasised rather than redeemed the general character of the cemetery ; one would not expect the graves of the inhabitants of a subject state to be very rich, and that the wealth of the First Dynasty was a thing of the past is shown perhaps most eloquently of all by the beads ; stones unknown or rare in the old days, agate, chalcedony, and hæmatite, now become relatively common, but when gold is used we find only too often, instead of the solid metal, copper beads plated with the thinnest gold. In face of this it is not surprising that the city contains no great buildings of the age.

It would have been difficult to date the Sargonid cemetery but for one of those chances which, improbable as they may seem, do occur to help the archæologist. No less than three cylinder seals have been found, two of them actually in intact graves and one loose in the soil, bearing inscriptions in which there is added to the owner's name the statement that he held office in the household of the very daughter of king Sargon—one was her hairdresser, one her scribe, and one her steward. An object discovered in the ruins of the Moon-goddess's temple explains the otherwise unaccountable fact of the presence of Sargon's daughter at Ur : it is a disk of alabaster—the moon's disk—on one side of which is a much-damaged relief showing a stepped altar, in front of which a priest is pouring libations ; behind the priest stands a female figure in long flounced garments, and behind her two attendants with offerings ; on the back is a written dedication by the daughter of Sargon.

Now, there is an inscription of Nabonidus, the last of the kings of Babylon, describing how he appointed his daughter High Priestess of the Moon-god at Ur, and the king states that in so doing he was following a precedent set by Kudur-Mabug, one of the Larsa

Kings, who had reigned some fifteen hundred years before—about 2000 B.C. Clearly, long before Kudur-Mabug's time, Sargon had done the same, and the limestone slab of the period of Entemena, which has been described above and bears precisely the same scene rendered by a more primitive art, carries the precedent further back still : all through history such importance attached to the great Temple of Nannar the Moon-god at Ur, and to the city as the main centre of his worship, that the reigning king, though a foreigner, might hold it worth his while to send his daughter as High Priestess there ; in one case at least a king's son was High Priest of the Moon-goddess.

Not only then can we date our graves accurately— king Sargon reigned from 2630 to 2575 B.C.—but we can establish a new fact reflecting the glory of the city even when it was not an imperial capital. It is indeed a strange coincidence which has preserved from a period so little represented in our excavations four separate monuments all connected with one person, and that the daughter of the outstanding figure of the age.

Chapter IV

The Great Days of the Third Dynasty

AT NO TIME IN ITS LONG HISTORY WAS THE CITY OF UR
so important as in the days of the Third Dynasty,
about 2300 B.C. to 2180 B.C., when it was the capital
of the Sumerian empire. The founder of the
dynasty was Ur-Nammu (or Ur-Engur, as the name
used to be written), and he founded a royal house of
which four generations after him were to sit upon
the throne ; he was a great conqueror and a great
ruler, famous for his justice and his good works,
whose dominions extended from the Persian Gulf
to the Mediterranean, and his monuments were
broadcast throughout the cities of Mesopotamia. It
is a curious fact that no literary texts of his reign or
of the reigns of his posterity survive, and that what
we know of him has to be pieced together from
scattered references and from the ruins of his
buildings.

Two fragmentary inscriptions on stone found in
the temple of the Moon-goddess throw some light
on the beginnings of his kingdom. Each of them
records the founding by Ur-Nammu of a temple or
shrine, but whereas nearly all Ur-Nammu's other
dedications are made to Nannar, the god of the city

of Ur, here the deities he honours are the patron
gods of the city of Erech, and he prays for the life of
Utu-khegal the king of Erech, calling himself only by
the title of ' governor.' Now, Erech was the seat of
the dynasty which in the king-lists precedes that of
Ur, and it is clear that when these temples were
built Ur-Nammu was a vassal of Utu-khegal ; it was
by rebellion against his master that he made himself
overlord of the empire.

When once he had established his position as
independent king Ur-Nammu showed himself an
indefatigable builder, but especially was he determined to make his own city worthy of its rank as
capital. Probably during the long period of subjection to foreign kings and the comparative poverty
which had resulted from that subjection the temples
of the gods had fallen into disrepair ; in any case,
they were old and out of date : the programme of
the new ruler provided for a virtual rebuilding of the
whole central part of the city.

What strikes one most about the extant work of
Ur-Nammu is its amazing solidity ; he seemed to
build for all time and shrank from no amount of
labour to that end, and it is no wonder that his
reign of eighteen years did not suffice for the
completion of all he planned. Last winter we carried

out some experimental work on the city walls and
discovered the substructure of the defences with
which Ur-Nammu encircled his capital. Rising
26 feet or more above the plain and acting as retain-
ing-wall to the platform on which the town buildings were raised, there was a rampart constructed of
unbaked brick throughout which at its base was no
less than 77 feet thick ! The wall proper, built of
baked brick, which ran along the top of the rampart,
has disappeared at the point where our trial excavations were made, but, judging from the unusually
large size of the bricks employed for it, it must have
been a very solid structure ; but even apart from
that, few kings would lightly embark on the task of
putting up a wall 77 feet thick around a space which
must measure some three-quarters of a mile in
length and nearly half a mile in width, yet this was
not the only work of Ur-Nammu and scarcely even
the greatest.

About seventy-five years ago Mr. J. E. Taylor,
then British Consul at Basra, was engaged by the
British Museum to investigate some of the ancient
sites of southern Mesopotamia, and amongst others
he visited Ur, in those days a place difficult and
dangerous of access. Struck by the obvious importance of one mound, which from its height,

overshadowing all the other ruins, he rightly judged to be the Ziggurat, he attacked it from above, cutting down into the brickwork of the four corners. The science of field archæology had not then been devised and the excavator's object was to find things that might enrich the cases of a museum, while the preservation of buildings on the spot was little considered. To the greatest monument of Ur Taylor did damage which we cannot but deplore to-day, but he succeeded in his purpose and at least made clear the importance of the site whose leter excavation has so well repaid us. Hidden in the brickwork of the top stage of the tower he found, at each angle of it, cylinders of baked clay on which were long inscriptions giving the history of the building. The texts date from about 550 B.C., from the time of Nabonidus, the last of the kings of Babylon, and state that the tower, founded by Ur-Nammu and his son Dungi, but left unfinished by them and not completed by any later king, he had restored and finished. These inscriptions not only gave us the first information obtained about the Ziggurat itself, but identified the site, called by the Arabs al Mughair, the Mound of Pitch, as Ur ' of the Chaldees,' the biblical home of Abraham.

Taylor's excavations did not go very far. Those

H

were the days when Rawlinson was unearthing in the north of Mesopotamia the colossal human-headed bulls and pictured wall-slabs which now enrich the British Museum, and dazzled by such discoveries people could not realise the value of the odds and ends which alone rewarded the explorer in the south : the site was deserted, and the upper stage of the Ziggurat which Taylor had exposed was left to the mercies of the weather and of Arab builders in search of cheap ready-made bricks, and when British troops advanced to Mughair in 1915 only a few bits of ragged brick showed at the corners of a mound up which a man could ride on horseback. In 1918 part of one end was cleared by Dr. Hall, and it was found that lower down the casing was wonderfully well preserved. In 1922–3 the excavation of the tower was seriously taken in hand and for two seasons employed a large number of our men, while work on the surrounding buildings was continued until 1929.

The amount of rubbish which had to be removed before the ruins of the tower stood free was very great, running into thousands of tons, and in all this mass we found scarcely any objects of interest. Near the surface of the lower part of the slope there were quantities of bricks covered with a bright blue glaze,

wreckage from the little shrine with which Nabonidus had crowned the ancient monument ; flung
down in a gateway at the back of the tower we found
the mutilated statue of Entemena to which reference
has already been made, and in front of the tower
fragments of an inscription on black stone, of late
date, recording the buying-up of various blocks of
house property for the enlargement of a temple ; but
otherwise we had to be content with the tower itself
as the result of our prolonged toil. And it was a
result well worth having. The top part, as we knew
beforehand, was the work of Nabonidus, but the
bulk of the construction was original, and on its
bricks could be read the name and title of the first
founder.

The Ziggurat is a peculiar feature of Sumerian
architecture and as such calls for explanation. I have
already said that we do not quite know who the
Sumerians are ; tradition would make them come
from the East ; the study of their bones and skulls
shows that they were a branch of the Indo-European
stock of the human race resembling what is called
Caucasian man, a people who in stature and in
appearance might pass as modern Europeans rather
than as Orientals. Geographically, it is likely that
their original homeland was in hilly country, and this

is made more likely by certain facts such as that
their gods are often represented standing upon
mountains and the animals pictured in their art are
often of a mountain type, while the evidence that
their temple architecture was really a translation
into brick of an original timber structure would
indicate that they had first learnt to build in a
wooded and therefore in a high-lying country.
People living in a mountainous land nearly always
associate their religion with the outstanding natural
features of that land and worship their gods on
' high places,' and this would seem to have been
true of the Sumerians. When they moved down into
the alluvial plain of the Euphrates they found themselves in a country where there were no hills meet
for the service of god, a country so flat that even a
private house, if it was to be safe from the periodic
inundations, had to be raised on an artificial platform. The latter fact supplied a hint as to how the
former difficulty could be solved : the platform had
only to be built high enough, and there, made by
man, was the high place which nature had failed to
provide ; and so the Sumerians set to work to build
—using ' bricks instead of stone, and slime (bitumen) had they for mortar '—a ' ziggurat ' whose
name might be called ' the Hill of Heaven ' or ' the

Mountain of God.' In every important city there was at least one such tower crowned by a sanctuary, the tower itself forming part of a larger temple complex ; of them all the biggest and the most famous was the Ziggurat of Babylon, which in Hebrew tradition became the Tower of Babel, now entirely destroyed, but its ground-plan shows that it was but a repetition on a larger scale of the Ziggurat at Ur, the best-preserved of all these monuments.

The Ziggurat stands at the back of the temple of Nannar the Moon-god, of which it is the main feature. The outer court of the temple was a terrace raised 10 feet or more above the level in front of it, and behind the court rose a second and higher terrace on which stood the sanctuary and the tower. The tower measures a little more than 200 feet in length by 150 feet in width, and its original height was about 70 feet ; the whole thing is one solid mass of brickwork, the core being of unbaked brick and the face a skin of baked brick set in bitumen, about 8 feet thick. The walls, relieved by shallow buttresses, are battered, or built with a pronounced inward slope, and stand some 50 feet high ; this forms the lowest stage. Above this point the tower is taken up in steps or stages each smaller than the one below, leaving narrow passages along the main

sides and wider terraces at either end ; but the stages
are curiously unsymmetrical, so that there are three
storeys at the north-west end of the building and
four at the south-east end, all communicating by
flights of brick stairs ; on the topmost storey, which
was virtually a square, stood the little shrine of the
god.

On three sides the walls rose sheer to the level of the
first terrace (Plate IX *a*), but on the north-east face
fronting the Nannar temple was the approach to
the shrine. Three brick stairways, each of a hundred
steps, led upwards, one projecting out at right angles
from the building, two leaning against its wall, and
all converging in a great gateway on the level of the
second terrace ; from this gate a single flight of
stairs ran straight up to the door of the shrine,
while lateral passages with smaller flights of stairs
gave access to the terraces at either end of the tower ;
the angles formed by the three main stairways were
filled in with solid flat-topped buttress-towers
(Plate IX *b*).

When first we started the work of drawing out the
plan and elevations of the Ziggurat we were puzzled
to find that the different measurements never seemed
to agree ; then it was discovered that in the whole
building there is not a single straight line, and that

what we had assumed to be such were in fact carefully calculated curves. The walls not only slope
inwards, but the line from top to bottom is slightly
convex ; on the ground plan the wall line from corner
to corner of the building has a distinct outward bend,
so that sighting along it one can only see as far as the
centre ; the architect has aimed at an optical illusion
which the Greek builders of the Parthenon at
Athens were to achieve many centuries afterwards,
the curves being so slight as not to be apparent, yet
enough to give to the eye an appearance of strength
where a straight line might by contrast with the
mass behind it have seemed incurved and weak. The
employment of such a device does great credit to the
builders of the twenty-third century before Christ.
Indeed, the whole design of the building is a
masterpiece. It would have been so easy to pile
rectangle of brickwork above rectangle, and the
effect would have been soulless and ugly ; as it is,
the heights of the different stages are skilfully calculated, the slope of the walls leads the eye upwards
and inwards to the centre, the sharper slope of the
triple staircase accentuates that of the walls and fixes
the attention on the shrine above, which was the
religious focus of the whole structure, while across
these converging lines cut the horizontal planes of

the terraces, the division of the building which
they effect being emphasised by zones of colour.
At least in the later period the lower stages were
painted black, the uppermost was red, and the
shrine, as we have seen, was covered with blue-
glazed tiles, and it is probable that the shrine roof
took the form of a dome of gilded metal : these
colours had their mystical significance and stood for
the various divisions of the universe, the dark underworld, the habitable earth, the heavens, and the sun.

No one looking at the Ziggurat can fail to notice
the tall and narrow slits which at regular intervals
and in rows one above another pierce the brickwork
of the walls ; they run clean through the burnt-brick
casing and deep into the mud brick of the core,
where they are loosely filled with broken pottery.
These are ' weeper-holes ' intended to drain the
interior, a necessary precaution, for with damp the
mud brick would swell and make the outer walls
bulge if it did not burst them altogether.

This is the obvious and correct explanation and for
a long time it satisfied us ; but then the difficulty
arose, how was the damp likely to get into the core ?
There was no real danger at the time of construction,
for though there would then be plenty of water in
the mud mortar used for the crude bricks, this would

dry—indeed, with so vast an area to build over, one course would be virtually dry before the next was laid above it—and the tendency of the core would be to shrink rather than to expand. It is true that torrential rains fall in Mesopotamia, but in the days of the Third Dynasty it was usual to lay pavements of burnt brick two, three, or even five courses thick set in bitumen mortar, and no surface water could penetrate this and do harm below. If there had been such a pavement, the precaution was needless; and if there was not such, why not? And further, at each end of the tower there is in one of the buttresses a deep recess in the brickwork running from the edge of the first terrace to the ground, and at the bottom of this there is what engineers call an ' apron,' a mass of brick waterproofed with bitumen and built with its top at a slant calculated to carry off smoothly and without splash water falling from above : evidently there was water on the terrace.

In the doorway of a room of late date lying against the back wall of the tower we found the great diorite hinge-stone bearing an inscription of Nabonidus in which he refers to his repairs of the building and states that he cleared the ' Gig-par-ku ' of fallen branches. As the excavations progressed we were able to establish that the Gig-par-ku was a part of the temple complex dedicated to the Moon-goddess, and that it lay close under the south-east end of the Ziggurat ; somehow the site of this building had become encumbered with branches of trees. There may have been trees in the Gig-par-ku itself, but as most of it was roofed in, this is not very likely ; and the only other place from which the branches could have fallen into it was the Ziggurat itself.

This explains the weeper-holes. The terraces of Ur-Nammu's staged tower were not paved with brick but were covered with soil, and in this trees were planted ; the long recesses in the buttresses may have carried off the waters of a violent storm, but they may equally have served as water-hoists for the irrigation of the terrace ; and what made possible the swelling of the core of the tower and therefore necessitated the weeper-holes in its facing was just this irrigation—the water poured at the roots of the trees would percolate through the top soil into the crude brick, and if it had no outlet would really endanger the building.

Thus we have to imagine trees clothing every terrace with greenery, hanging gardens which brought more vividly to mind the original conception of the Ziggurat as the Mountain of God, and we shall recognise how much better the sloping outer walls harmonise with this conception, rising as they do like the abrupt bare sides of some pine-topped crag, than if they had been uncompromisingly vertical, the walls of a house of man's building.

With the destruction of the upper storey there is nothing left to show the character of the shrine as built by Ur-Nammu, but from what does remain we can see how splendid a monument his Ziggurat was and how well adapted for the use of those processions which formed a part of Sumerian religious ritual ; the priests in robes of state bearing the statue and emblem of Nannar up and down the triple staircase against the background of coloured brick and trees must have made a magnificent spectacle, and it is easy to think that some tradition of these great feast-days was at the bottom of the vision which showed to Jacob ladders set up to Heaven and the angels ascending and descending on them. Yet the tower was only one part of the Temple of Nannar. Against one side of it lay the sanctuary of that temple, and in front of it, at a lower level, stretched the great court, a paved space some ninety yards across surrounded with chambers and store-rooms and entered by a triple gate passing under a high gate tower. The excavation of this has taken us a long time, and the temple had .been so often altered and repaired that not much of the original founder's work survives, but its plan and a good deal of its history have come to light.

The walls which we first found when we came to dig deep along the confines of the temple were not those of the Third Dynasty at all ; we got down to the foundations of the terrace and yet no sign of them appeared, and it looked as if they had been completely destroyed. Then it was found that a king reigning about three hundred years after Ur-Nammu had enlarged the terrace on which the court of the temple stands and had built a new retaining wall outside the old and, filling up the space between them with rubbish, had erected his new flanking chambers along the edge of the wider platform : we had to dig through the floors of these chambers to find the buried remains of the old terrace wall.

When it was found, a fresh problem arose : the lower section of the wall which supported the terrace was of mud bricks whose size proved them to be of Third Dynasty date, but they bore no stamp of authorship ; such of the superstructure as was left, the walls of the range of rooms built along the terrace edge and enclosing the courtyard, were of burnt bricks stamped with the name not of Ur-Nammu but of his son Dungi. The bricks of the Ziggurat bear Ur-Nammu's name exclusively, the Ziggurat is part of the temple, and until the lower terrace of the courtyard was built the construction of the Ziggurat terrace and of the Ziggurat itself could not have been begun ; therefore the mud-brick wall upholding the courtyard terrace must have been the work of Ur-Nammu. The inscribed cylinders of Nabonidus found by Taylor in the upper brickwork of the tower state that it was built by Ur-Nammu and his son Dungi ; in the Ziggurat itself we have found no trace of Dungi's work, but since tower and temple are essentially one we can apply the statement to the whole building and see how well it harmonises with discovered facts.

Ur-Nammu started, as he was bound to do, with the substructures, the lower terrace which was to be the courtyard area, the higher terrace which was to be the platform for the temple sanctuary and the Ziggurat. As soon as that was done, he concentrated all his efforts on the sanctuary (where we find his brick-stamps commonly) and on the great tower, and so far as the evidence of the ruins goes he finished both these ; then, before the walls of the outer court had risen above ground-level, the king died. Probably the early part of his reign of eighteen

years had been spent in war, and during most of it
he may have been absent from his capital and not
so firmly established that he could afford to spend
much time and money on bricks and mortar;
certainly his building activity seems to have been
confined rather to his later years and had been
deferred too long; the temple of Nannar is not the
only case at Ur where we have found the father's
work completed by the son. In this case it was the
outer court which Dungi had to build, and the fact
of the divided authorship enables us to date the
building with unusual precision—the scanty relics
of burnt-brick construction which define the outlines of the court chambers belong to the very first
years of the reign of the new king.

Very little of his work is preserved, and it would
have been impossible to make out even its ground-
plan but for the pious conservativism which Mesopotamian rulers observed in most of their dealings
with temples; however thorough might be the
repairs required, even though they amounted to the
complete reconstruction of the fabric, the restorers
were nearly always at pains to reproduce as nearly
as might be the general lay-out of the old building.
Very often they would raze the old walls but leave in
position one course of bricks to serve as a guide to

the new builders, and when such reconstruction has been repeated more than once we may find in the lowest four or five courses of the standing walls bricks stamped with the names of three or four kings of different dates, giving with each course a fresh chapter in the life-history of the temple. Here Dungi's walls had not been used as a substructure for the new building, but were buried uselessly beneath its floors, hacked away and cut across in every direction by the labourers who dug the trenches for the foundations of the larger temple, but just enough was preserved to prove that the new work did reproduce, though on a larger scale and in a more ornate form, the Third Dynasty model, and we could with full confidence complete on paper a plan which in the field was represented only by fragments of brickwork, shapeless and at first sight without meaning.

When we were clearing the ruins of the sanctuary lying under the shadow of the Ziggurat on its north-west side we found, re-used as hinge-sockets in a later doorway, two fragments of limestone carved in relief ; in the courtyard of the temple Dublal-makh, some hundred and fifty yards away to the south-east, more carved fragments were discovered which actually fitted on to the first two, and another piece apparently belonging to the same monument turned up in the ruins of yet another temple, E-Nun-makh.

The fragments found thus widely scattered made up a considerable part of a limestone stela which originally measured 5 feet across and may have been as much as 15 feet high. It was sculptured on both sides and recorded in pictorial and in written form the achievements of Ur-Nammu. One scene at least commemorated the king's exploits in war, for we have him seated on his throne while prisoners with bound hands are led before him ; two scenes show sacrifice to the gods ; two panels, practically identical, are of a more unusual sort—the king is represented standing in the attitude of prayer, while an angel flying down from above pours water on to the ground from a vase held between his hands (Plate X a). An inscription giving a list of the canals in the neighbourhood of Ur dug by orders of the king explains the scene : Ur-Nammu has been responsible for the actual earth-work of the canals, but he assigns to the gods credit for the blessed gift of water which brings fertility to the land. It is a pleasing instance of modesty in a great king, and the earliest representation of an angel in art.

But there was another act of which Ur-Nammu seems to have been particularly proud, seeing that to it were devoted no less than three distinct panels of the relief, and that is the construction of the Ziggurat. In one scene the ruler is shown twice over making libations, on the one side to Nannar and on the other side to his wife the goddess Nin-Gal, and Nannar holds out to him the measuring-rod and coiled line of the architect, thereby symbolising his wish that Ur-Nammu should build him a house (Plate X *b*). In the next scene, sadly incomplete, the king obediently presents himself before the god bearing on his shoulder the tools of the architect and of the builder, compasses, mortar-basket, pick and trowel ; in a third, yet more fragmentary, the workmen are seen carrying hods of mortar up ladders and laying the bricks of the tower. It is an extraordinary chance which has given us together with the best preserved of all the ziggurats of Mesopotamia the contemporary record of its building, and scarcely less extraordinary was the chance which brought together fragments deliberately smashed and so widely scattered. The monument is still very far from complete, but at any moment we may discover fresh bits of what is undoubtedly the most important sculpture known from Ur.

The Ziggurat was itself so solidly built that we need

not be surprised if it stood almost unaltered and unrepaired for seventeen hundred and fifty years, but the Nannar Temple underwent in that time many changes. In the courtyard we can trace various modifications some of which date from very little later than the time of Dungi its joint founder : new altars were erected ; at one end there was built what seems to have been a miniature ziggurat with a secret chamber hidden in the heart of its brickwork ; and then came the enlargement which has already been described. One feature of the new temple deserves special mention, for it was peculiar in itself and was to be copied by future restorers : the outer façade and the wall dividing the court from the sanctuary were decorated with brick half-columns, down the centre of which ran double grooves or recesses ; this scheme of ornament, which belonged to the temple standing in Abraham's time, is in striking contrast to the normal Sumerian tradition of rectangles and heavy masses almost unrelieved and must have given to the building a grace quite new to the architects of Ur.

About six hundred years after this reconstruction the temple of Nannar had become so ruinous that the king who then reigned at Babylon and was overlord of the south country also razed its walls to the

ground and built them afresh ; for the outer façade
he preferred a simpler style, plainly rectangular, but
perhaps not less impressive ; square buttresses with
complicated re-entrant angles were set regularly
along the front of the building with a deeper pro-
jection towards the centre, where there stood out
boldly a huge gate-tower higher and more massive
than that of former days ; only inside the court the
front wall of the sanctuary imitated with its rows of
half-columns the work of six centuries before.

In about 650 B.C. fresh reconstruction was called
for. During the preceding age various kings had carried out minor repairs, and we find new pavements
of burnt brick laid down, the bricks stamped with
the king's name, and old pavements patched with
bricks nameless or borrowed from some other work ;
but now the governor who ruled Ur in the name of
the king of Assyria was obliged by the state of the
chief temple of the city to embark on a more
thorough-going restoration. It is eloquent of the low
estate on which Ur had fallen in these latter days
that the Assyrian's work should have been of so
shoddy a character ; where he employed burnt
bricks for wall foundations they were old material
collected from the ruins, mere house-breakers'
rubbish, and all his new buildings were in mud

brick disguised by plaster and whitewash, while his floors were but of beaten mud.

When we started digging out the temple, the very first wall encountered was that of the Assyrian period dividing the court from the sanctuary, and at first it puzzled us not a little. Close below the modern surface a mud-brick wall was found and the pickman was ordered to follow it along ; it ran straight for perhaps a yard, then took four right-angled turns in the length of a foot, then swelled out in a bold curve which after 2 feet or so was broken by the eight angles of a double recess and continued in a fresh curve back to the original line, only to curve out again as before. The workman, hard put to it to distinguish the crumbling brick at all, was further bewildered by these seemingly inconsequential meanderings of what ought to have been a straight face, and reported that the wall was mad. Mistrusting his work, for it is only too easy for a man armed with a pick to carve the soft mud brick into a shape quite other than that which the builder gave it, I ordered him to retrace his steps and dig deeper to a level at which the bricks might be better preserved ; he did so, and at a depth to which the rain-water did not penetrate to rot the brickwork found the wall with its coating of mud plaster and whitewash, pitted indeed by the ravages of the white ant, but almost intact.

It was the wall built by Sin-balatsu-ikbi the Assyrian more than 2,500 years ago, with its row of half-columns and recesses copied from a model nearly 1,500 years older still, and the whitewash was no worse than one might see on any modern house in the nearest market-town of Iraq ; it was crumbly, and a touch would flake it off, but it was the pride of our Arab pickmen to use their tools so delicately that the columns freed from the earth glistened white, and though the rains of one winter washed away virtually every trace of whitewash and mortar and reduced the sharp angles and curves of the brickwork to a shapeless wavy line, yet we have photographs in which the lower part of the wall at least looks much as it did when the Assyrians were masters of Ur.

One good reason for the wonderful preservation of the whitewash was that the walls had not stood very long above ground. Within fifty years of their being built, the lower part of them had been protected by a solid casing of earth. Nebuchadnezzar, who was king of Babylon about 600 B.C., once more repaired the Nannar temple, and part of his scheme was to bring the forecourt and the sanctuary to one level by

raising the former ; masses of soil were heaped over
Sin-balatsu-ikbi's mud floor and a new brick pavement was laid down over this. Using the buried
footing of the old walls as a foundation, he built new
walls in mud brick with doorways at the new level,
sank a well at one end of the court so as to have a
handy supply of water for the temple rites, and then
remodelled the sanctuary also, adding to it another
wing on the south-east side of the Ziggurat and
putting here a shrine which, judging from the long
narrow brick base occupying the greater part of the
chamber, was a ' boat shrine ' containing the model
of the ship in which the Moon-god crossed the sky
—that high-prowed and high-sterned ship which is
so like the moon's crescent.

This was the last transformation which the ancient
temple was to undergo ; no other royal builder interested himself in it, and before very long, when
the Persian conquerors of Mesopotamia changed
their religion and adopted Zoroastrianism with its
worship of unembodied fire, Nannar's great house,
like all the old temples, was doomed to destruction.
Of Nebuchadnezzar's work very little survives to-
day, only a few patches of brick pavement almost
flush with the modern surface, a few bricks of the
walls and, deeper underground, the brick boxes

which shelter the hinge-stones of the doors and prove by their position against the jambs of the buried doors of the Assyrian that Nebuchadnezzar's temple followed the lines of its predecessor : very little, but just enough to complete the life history of the most famous of the temples of Ur.

From the sixth century B.C. back to the twenty-third we have traced the evidence of reconstruction and repair and have laid bare what remains of the great building which Ur-Nammu planned and did not live to finish ; but underneath that there is still made soil and in it enough to prove that the Third Dynasty temple was not the first to occupy the site, though of what went before it we shall never know much. In the courtyard we found only a few bricks of that ' plano-convex ' type which goes back to the fourth millennium before Christ ; but when we were following up the back wall of the temple enceinte which runs along the edge of the platform behind the Ziggurat, we came on more decisive evidence.

Inside Ur-Nammu's wall and parallel with it there ran underground, buried in the filling of the platform, a wall of mud bricks, slightly round-topped, though not quite of the type of those of the First Dynasty of Ur, which were laid not flat but on edge and slantwise, herringbone fashion. Experience shows that this peculiar style of building belongs to a period between the First and the Third dynasties, and provisionally we may assign it to that Second Dynasty of Ur about which in fact we know nothing at all. The herringbone wall not only is parallel to the later but shows traces of cross-walls belonging to a range of chambers exactly like the chambers in the double platform-wall of Ur-Nammu and his successors ; it is an earlier version of the same thing and it must have had the same purpose, i.e. it enclosed a terrace on which stood a ziggurat and a temple of Nannar.

That there should have been a ziggurat at Ur before the days of Ur-Nammu is a foregone conclusion, for so important a city as Ur could not have but possessed, from the earliest time, one of those staged towers which were typical of Sumerian architecture ; now we know precisely where it stood. Underneath the vast bulk of the Ziggurat which we see to-day there lies whatever may remain of an older and a smaller tower : built probably as early as the reign of Mes-anni-pad-da and repaired, as can be assumed from the existence of the mud-brick wall, by some nameless king of the Second Dynasty, the old ziggurat was used by Ur-Nammu as a foundation for his more ambitious building and either buried beneath the level of his new terrace or, more probably, embedded in the core of his tower. It would be a crime on our part to destroy one of the principal monuments of Iraq merely to prove the existence of what we know must have existed, and the chance is slight that we should find any such treasures as enriched the platform of the temple at al 'Ubaid, which in like fashion was buried beneath a new platform built by king Dungi : here theory must suffice, for we shall never see the older Ziggurat of Ur.

In describing the temple I have more than once had occasion to mention the hinge-sockets of the doors, and the phrase calls for explanation. The Sumerian door consisted of a wooden leaf fixed to a pole rather higher than itself ; the top end of the pole was held by a metal ring projecting from the corner of the door lintel and revolved in it ; the lower end was shod with metal and went down through a hole in the pavement to rest and turn on the hinge-stone. This was a boulder of imported hard stone, limestone or diorite, in which a cup-shaped hollow had been cut to take the pole-shoe, and generally one part of it (when the door was that of a temple) had been smoothed and inscribed with the name of the king who dedicated the building and of the god in whose honour he built it.

Door-sockets are thus invaluable evidence for the date and nature of the buildings we unearth ; they have to be used with caution, because imported stones were valuable and an old socket would often be taken away and re-used for some other building than that for which it was first intended and the old inscription may no longer apply, but even so the text may yield new facts, and where the stone is certainly in its original position the information it gives may be invaluable. Without such inscriptions it would have been impossible to identify the sanctuary of the Nannar temple and so to complete its ground-plan ; we had not suspected its position and had no notion of the form it might assume, and the walls of the Ur-Nammu building were so terribly ruined, seldom standing at all above floor level, that at first little could be made of them. The door-sockets lying below floor-level and therefore undisturbed bore the inscription ' the House of Nannar,' and from their position on the wall-line we could fix the whereabouts of the chamber doors, thus giving sense to the plan.

One furnished us with a new experience. The wall had vanished and only part of the bitumen-covered brick pavement was left, but in it was a square hole filled with earth ; going down into this we found not only the block of diorite with Ur-Nammu's inscription but, still standing upright in the worn cup-like hollow in which it had once revolved, the copper shoe of the hinge-pole with a duplicate inscription on its side. The contrast between the complete destruction of the building above ground and the preservation of the hinge which had not even lost its balance on the stone could not but impress one.

At the far end of what we call the Sacred Area, the enclosure which contained the various buildings dedicated to the Moon-god or to the minor deities associated with him, there is another building of king Ur-Nammu. Part of this was excavated seventy years ago by Taylor, and where he dug very little of the structure survives to-day ; another part was excavated by Dr. Hall, and the final clearing was done by the Joint Expedition. Dr. Hall found that the paved floors were of bricks stamped with the name of Dungi and giving the name of the building as ' the House of the Mountain,' apparently a palace. When we dug here we found that the bricks of the actual walls were stamped with Ur-Nammu's name and the title of the building was merely ' the House of Nannar,' which might apply to almost any section of the Sacred Area.

Here there was a contradiction which had to be

straightened out, so we searched the corners of the
building for a ' foundation-deposit ' and duly
found what we had hoped for : built into the wall
foundations at each corner there was a box of burnt
bricks lined with matting and waterproofed with
bitumen, and in each box there stood a copper object
of which the upper half was a human figure from
the waist upwards and the lower half more like a
nail or cone ; the figure was that of the royal founder
presented in the guise of a temple servant or
labourer bearing on his head a basket of mortar : in
front of the figure there lay a small stone cut into
the shape of a brick, the foundation-stone of the
building. It was the regular custom at this period
in Sumerian history to bury such statuettes and
stones in the foundation-boxes, and the king's name
and the name of the temple were recorded on the
front of the figure and on the polished surface of the
stone. What was, then, our dismay when, having
looked to these very objects to solve all our difficulties, we found them absolutely blank ! There
was nothing to show whether the statuette represented Dungi or Ur-Nammu, whether the building
were a palace or a temple. Then we had recourse to
the doorways, and at every one we found a socket-
stone in place, and not one bore a sign of inscription.

As the clearing of the building progressed its resemblance to the normal temple became more and more clear. At one end there was an entrance leading into a wide but shallow court from which a double gateway flanked by what seemed to be purification-chambers gave access to the main or inner court ; on the far side of this two doors led through little antechambers into a long room which corresponded exactly with the sanctuary or Holy of Holies in other temples close by. A heavy wall running right through the building separated the ' temple ' part from a complex of chambers clearly of a more domestic nature and divided into two apparently residential units each consisting of rooms grouped about an open central court ; one of the groups was reached directly by a doorway from the inner court of the ' temple,' the other only by a winding passage and double doors from the ' sanctuary.' Most temples contained residential quarters for the priests, and therefore everything in the arrangement of this building agreed with its identification as a temple. But as against this there was the ambiguity of the texts on the bricks of the floor and the walls respectively, the uncompromising blankness of the foundation-figures, which ought to have been inscribed, and the equal blankness of the door-sockets—and we have never yet found a temple in which none of the door-stones bore an inscription. It was an archæological problem to which perhaps no final solution can be given, but one which the archæologist ought to do his best to solve so far as the evidence allows.

The contradiction in the question of authorship presents no great difficulty. The walls of a building must be put up before the floors are laid, and the two operations need not be the work of one person. Ur-Nammu built the walls and then died, leaving the building unfinished as he had left unfinished the Temple of Nannar, and his son Dungi put the final touches to it. Ur-Nammu calls it the ' House of Nannar,' which need mean no more than that it formed part of the group of religious foundations under the patronage of the god ; Dungi may possibly have used for the floors bricks manufactured for another building whose site we have not yet discovered, but there is no need to assume this, and his name ' the House of the Mountain ' may quite well be the particular name of the building more vaguely described by his father. Copper foundation-figures such as we found in the corner boxes were, so far as we know, only used for religious buildings, but then they are generally inscribed, and the fact that here they are not is against the building being really a temple, and the same is true of the door-sockets. The answer may be given by the ground-plan, which is so like that of a temple that it almost proves the building to be something else.

We know that according to Sumerian beliefs a king was the vice-gerent of god upon earth—' tenant-farmer,' they called him—and that the god was the real ruler of the land. The god then being the king, his court exactly reproduced that of his human representative. Attached to the principal temple there would be ministers of War and Justice, of Communications, of Agriculture, of Finance, of the Harem, and so on ; and as with the personnel, so it was with the house in which the visible statue of him was lodged : in the sanctuary he received the adoration of those who might approach him, but he also had his bed-chamber, his place for dining, and necessarily, too, rooms and offices in which the business of his temple and estates could be carried on. It is most probable that in the details of its arrangements a great temple, which was the House of God, afforded a close parallel to the palace which was the house of the king. We have many examples of temples and none hitherto of palaces, but because Ur-Nammu's building is so like a temple I think that we may accept Dungi's name for it and take it to be the palace of the kings of Ur.

If that be so, we might hazard an explanation of the copper statuettes. The Sumerian kings claimed divine powers and were deified in their lifetimes, so that the royal palace would fittingly be placed within the Sacred Area under Nannar's protection and its founding might well be marked by the same ritual as that of a temple ; but where the building was in the king's own honour there would be a difficulty about the inscription on his statuette, and it might be omitted. We have never found an inscribed door-socket in a private house, and here the blank stone may mean that in Dungi's mind, as his brick inscriptions show, the idea of the palace of the earthly king overshadowed that of the house of god's vice-gerent himself deified.

Certainly in this light we can interpret the building satisfactorily. The temple-like section comprises the public reception rooms where the ruler, seated on his throne in the long back room, just like the god on his pedestal in the sanctuary, gave audience to his subjects gathered in the inner court ; the two groups of residential quarters were for the king and his women-folk respectively, and the difference between them agrees well with this, one being easy

PLATE IX

(*a*) The south-west face of Ur-Nammu's Ziggurat.

(*b*) The Ziggurat restored.

PLATE X

(*a*) The angel pours out water on the earth.

(*b*) The King receives the order to build the Ziggurat.
The Stela of Ur-Nammu.

of access, while the harem-rooms are hidden away and hard to come to.

I have gone at length into this subject because the interpretation of evidence is not the least important part of the field-worker's task, and I have chosen a problem to which the answer is not certain because it illustrates better the kind of difficulty which one encounters nearly every day and generally forgets as soon as it is solved. If the identification of the building which I have suggested is correct, it adds much to its interest, for it is no small thing to possess the ruins of the actual house of the greatest of the kings of Ur.

K

Chapter V

The Buildings of the Larsa Kings

THE SPLENDOUR OF THE THIRD DYNASTY OF UR WENT out in shame and disaster. The sturdy mountaineers of Persia swept over the river-valley, the Sumerian forces were beaten in the field, the king of Ur was carried away captive, and when the Elamites returned to their hills they left behind them a wasted land with its temples overthrown and its cities in ruins. Ur, as the capital of the empire, must have borne the brunt of calamity and could not easily recover ; when the Sumerians again lifted up their heads it was another city which took the lead, and the kings of Isin and Larsa, once vassal states, became in turn the overlords of Sumer.

But tradition was too strong for these ' foreign ' rulers to neglect the old capital and the seat of the Moon-god's worship, and we find that not only were they active in repairing the damage wrought by the Elamites, so that most of the important buildings contain bricks stamped with the names of one or other of the Isin and Larsa kings, but the last king of Isin put his own son at Ur as high priest of the Moon-goddess Nin-Gal. This royal priest must have been something of a diplomat, for when his father lost his throne and the overlordship passed to the rival state of Larsa, he still managed to keep his position ; that he also prospered in it is clear from the great buildings which he set up, but in his inscriptions he is careful to explain that these are offerings to the gods for the life of the Larsa king.

The temple of Nin-Gal had been built by Ur-Nammu's grandson, but it was only of crude mud brick and we may suppose that it had suffered much at the hands of the Elamite invaders ; in any case, Enannatum the priest determined to rebuild it on the old lines but in better material. Excavating the site, we found his building standing on the stumps of the older walls which had been used by the new bricklayers as a foundation, and so recovered at one time the ground-plan of both temples.

The building was a rectangle measuring 240 feet either way, and was surrounded by an enormously heavy wall through the heart of which a narrow paved corridor ran round three sides of it, leading from a gate-tower over the main entrance to two fortified towers at the far corners ; a similar corridor cut straight across the building, dividing it into two unequal parts and affording quick access from one tower to the other. From the outside at least the temple must have looked more like a military than a

religious structure. Inside, however, its purpose
was unmistakable. The larger section was again
subdivided by a cross-wall, on one side of which was
a complete temple lying just inside the main entrance
and on the other minor shrines and living-quarters
for the priests.

The temple, with its outer and inner court, its two
little antechambers and its long shallow sanctuary,
was identical in its arrangement with the audience-
hall of Ur-Nammu's palace. At the same time it
presented certain curious features. Between the
outer and the inner court were two long chambers,
of which the first had a wide doorway opening on to
the outer court, and against the back wall, facing the
door, a brick base for a statue ; it looked as if this
was a ' Court of the Gentiles ' to which the general
public would be admitted to pay their devotions
before the statue in the half-way shrine, while the
inner court was reserved for the priests. To reach
this one passed through the second narrow chamber,
round which ran a raised brick bench waterproofed
with bitumen and having along its edge a runnel for
water ; the floor also was covered with bitumen and
sloped gently to the door leading to a tiny room in
the centre of which was a terra-cotta drain going
deep down into the earth. Obviously this was a

lustral chamber, and here the worshipper would purify himself before going farther on to holy ground. The inner court and the sanctuary had been terribly ruined, but enough remained of them to show the place of the great altar of sacrifice in the court and inside the sanctuary the bases of the statues, the stepped altar, and the ' vestry ' or treasury adjoining, while behind the sanctuary was the long passage-like chamber from which it is supposed that the priests worked the oracle.

In all this part, and in the next section of the building, excavation was made difficult by the presence of later walls whose foundations went down nearly as deep as the old work, while in some places the old floor-level had actually been re-used and the new walls simply set on the existing brick pavement. It was no easy matter to unravel the tangle of ruinous brickwork and to assign each fragment to its proper period, but when this was done the early plan was found to be remarkably regular and what had seemed mere confusion took on a very definite character.

The residential quarters of the priests were the most ruined of all, for there had been here a motive for more thorough-going destruction. In accordance with the fashion of the time the priests had been buried beneath the floors of their houses, and the brick vaults must have contained riches which tempted the avarice of the enemy who plundered the temple. In every case the pavements had been dug up and the tombs broken into and rifled so completely that there was scarcely anything over-looked—indeed, the only object worth mentioning which we found was a human face in glazed frit. Interesting in itself as being one of the earliest examples of polychrome glaze discovered in Mesopo-tamia, it was a tantalising sample of what the graves must once have contained, for the little statue from which it had been broken off was probably a rich and elaborate work of art.

Next to the living-quarters we found, very much better preserved, a building of a quite novel sort. From the corridor which ran through the temple precincts there opened off a narrow passage between blank walls with a door at the farther end ; going through the door, one found oneself in a similar and parallel passage leading in the opposite direc-tion, again with one door at the far end of the side wall ; this took one across a narrow room and down two more passages back into the corridor : it was a regular little maze of which the long central room contained the secret. Standing between its two doors, one looked down the length of a chamber, now of course roofless and with undecorated brick walls standing only some 5 feet high. The pavement was of brick, but the farther half of it was covered with bitumen on whose surface could be distinguished the impress of the reed mats which had once been spread there. Standing upright above the pavement, in which it was firmly bedded, was a large slab of white limestone, once round-topped, and side by side at its foot there lay fixed into the bitumen of the floor two other round-topped slabs of grey marble (Plate XI *a*), and on each of the three stones, in characters intentionally defaced but still legible, there was an inscription which read ' Bur-Sin king of Ur, king of Sumer and Akkad, king of the Four Quarters of the Earth, has built this to his lady Nin-Gal.' Against a side wall there was a low bench or table of bricks, and that was all.

What it meant was beyond doubt. The temple of the priest Enannatum reproduced exactly the older temple founded by Bur-Sin ; in that there had been a little sanctuary set aside for the worship of the royal founder, who was also a god. When the Third Dynasty came to an end and the Elamites sacked Ur, they broke up the sanctuary and tried to erase the name of the king, but Enannatum, repairing the building, repaired the shrine also and set up once more the dishonoured stones. Probably a statue of the king was enthroned against the upright stone, and on either side of it would be set poles capped with the symbols of power, mace-heads and the heads of beasts ; offerings would have their place on the brick table and walls and floor would be gay with hangings and rugs ; the pious would come down the winding passages and, pausing at the far end of the shrine, would pay their homage to the memory of the deified ruler. The shrine is dismantled now, of necessity, for the exposed ruins at Ur crumble in the rain and wind and are shrouded again in drifting sand ; but the whole chamber has been reconstructed in the Museum at Baghdad, and stands there unique evidence of the divine honours paid to Sumerian kings.

The rest of the great four-square building beyond the cross corridor consisted of a second temple of a different pattern. From the main court three arched doorways led to the sanctuary, where the statue of the goddess set on a high brick base looked out to the court. All round and behind the sanctuary were service chambers and magazines devoted to various uses. In one a queerly-shaped pit sunk in the pavement puzzled us until modern analogy proved that it was a weaver's pit, wherein the weaver sits with his legs below floor-level while he works at his low loom. Another set of rooms formed the kitchen : in an open court there was a well, and by it a bitumen-proofed tank for water, and a big copper ring let into the pavement was for the rope, so that the bucket might not be lost down the well ; against one wall were two fireplaces for boiling water, and against another the brick ' cutting-up table,' the criss-cross marks of the butcher's knife clearly visible on its top ; in a side-room was the beehive-shaped oven for baking bread, and in another room the cooking-range with two furnaces and circular flues, and in the flat top of it rings of small holes where the cauldrons were to be set : after thirty-eight centuries one could yet light the fires and reconstruct with all its activities the oldest kitchen in the world.

But it was the sanctuary and the courtyard that gave us the best results. We had been a long time getting down to them, for close under the surface there were remains of the late Babylonian period which had to be planned and noted before they could be removed, and they were so fragmentary that we were hard put to it to make sense of them. The mud-brick walls had vanished and only broken pavements survived in patches, and it was hard to

see where any one room began and ended. We had
done our best and started to pull up the floors when
a discovery was made which completed or confirmed
the rather theoretical ground-plan we had evolved.
Along every wall was a row of brick boxes placed
immediately below the pavement, so that a pavement brick formed the lid of each ; three bricks
set on end made the box, whose fourth side, facing
inwards to the room, was left open, and in each
sentry-box stood a roughly modelled and painted
figure of unbaked clay.   There were snakes and dogs
and gryphons, human figures and figures of men with
the heads of lions or bulls, with bulls' legs or fishes'
bodies, every sort of kindly demon that might guard
the house and keep off sickness or ill-luck (Plate
XIV *a*, facing p. 175) ; and with each there was a bit
of bone or a few calcined grains of barley, the relic
of the feast that had been made when the guardians
were put in their places. Cuneiform texts tell us
about these figures and of the ceremony of their
instalment with mystic formulæ and prayers ; now
we had actually found them still on duty, and they
preserved for us at least the outline of the house.

Below this more shoddy buildings had to be removed, and then we came on a series of fairly massive
mud-brick walls which proved to be those of a great

house built probably for the temple priests in about
1400 B.C., with separate dwellings all giving on a
central court. We were still high up in the mound,
some 6 feet or more above the level of the pavements of Enannatum's temple, and this was a good
sign. In this part of the building the walls, except
for the open space of the courtyard, were close
together, enclosing small chambers, and the walls
were very thick ; consequently when the upper
parts of them were overthrown, the debris filled the
rooms to a considerable height and the builders of
the succeeding age could not be bothered to remove
it ; it was simpler to build on the top of the mounds
and where the old court left a low-lying hollow to
put in a flight of brick steps down to it. Thus we
found the walls of the chambers round the sanctuary
standing 6 feet high and the fallen rubble between
them undisturbed, and as we went down through
this we were delighted to come across a layer of
ashes and burnt wood spread over the entire area.

Nothing helps an excavator like violent destruction.
If a building has fallen slowly into decay, one can be
sure that the impoverished inhabitants have removed
everything of value. The best thing that can happen
is a volcanic eruption which buries a place so
deeply that nobody goes back to salve his belongings ;

but the ideal conditions of a Pompeii are seldom met with, and one must be thankful for smaller mercies. If an enemy sacks a temple or a town, he is sure to overlook some objects at least which were of small intrinsic value for him, but may be very precious for the archæologist; and if he was so considerate as to set fire to the place and overthrow its walls, there is the further probability that his search was hurried and that no one else troubled to look for what he left behind.

So it was here. The ashes represented the ceilings and the panelling of the walls, and below them, lying on the brick pavement, there were hundreds of fragments of alabaster and soapstone vases and splinters of broken statues. One small statue we found entire, a heavy and clumsy figure carved in black stone representing the goddess Bau seated on a throne supported by geese; only her nose (which was made separately) was missing, and round the head were the small drilled holes to secure the gold crown which the robbers had torn off before discarding the statue. Bau was the patroness of the poultry farm, and this figure of her in its flounced and pleated dress reaching to the ankles, squat and thick-set, has an appropriately domestic look; it is far from being a first-class work of art, but as it is one of the very few Sumerian female statues in the round which time has preserved to us, it must rank high amongst our discoveries.

More fragmentary, for most of the head had vanished, but it was of far finer work, was a little seated figure of Nin-Gal herself, which bore a long inscription stating that it had been dedicated by no less a person than the priest Enannatum, the second founder of the temple. This was pieced together from many fragments widely scattered. As the splinters of stone were collected and cleaned there began a regular jig-saw game, and it was most exciting to watch them gradually growing up into complete vessels, sometimes inscribed with the names of ancient kings. A Sumerian temple, like a modern cathedral, was a veritable museum of antiquities; for centuries pious kings and others had been offering their treasures for the service of the god, and the temple strong-rooms would contain objects of all ages. It was here that we found the alabaster lunar disk of Sargon's daughter, and here too the limestone relief showing sacrifice being done by a princess of much older date—the latter was nearly a thousand years old and the former seven hundred when the robbers broke into the treasury where both were preserved.

One object was of peculiar interest. We found part

of a stone cup inscribed with a dedication by the daughter of king Dungi, herself a high priestess of the Moon-god ; another cup fragment bore the name of Sargon of Akkad, the great king who reigned 350 years before Dungi ; and then it was found that the two fragments joined together and that both inscriptions belonged to one and the same cup. How it came about that the princess owned what had been so long before the property of king Sargon we cannot tell, but that she did so is another proof of the way in which in the ancient as in the modern world objects might long survive their generation : we shall see later how another royal priestess of Ur indulged in a passion for ' antiques.'

The stone fragments lay thickest in the neighbourhood of the sanctuary, but in the courtyard also they were fairly abundant : at one end of this we found bits, unfortunately not very numerous, of a large alabaster slab inscribed with a list of the royal benefactions which had enriched the temple, and in the middle of the court scanty remains of a much more interesting document. There stood here a big base of solid brick, and on it and round it we picked up pieces of fine-grained black stone covered with inscription ; clearly the stone had originally been erected on the base, and enough remained of the text to show that it enumerated the conquests of the famous king and law-giver, Hammurabi of Babylon, that Amraphael who is mentioned in the fourteenth chapter of Genesis as a contemporary of Abraham : Hammurabi reduced Ur to subjection, and this was his war memorial set up in one of the chief temples of the city (Plate XI *b*).

Scattered at random in the chambers of the temple we found a number of inscribed clay tablets, part of the ordinary business records of the building. Such tablets are very often dated by the years of the reigning king, and on these we had represented most of the kings of Larsa, several years of Hammurabi, and the reign of his son almost continuously down to the eleventh year, and that was the last of the series. Now, the eleventh year was marked by a rebellion of the southern cities against Babylon, and the twelfth year was named ' that in which the king destroyed the walls of Ur ' ; here, then, we had a fixed date and a touch of drama. Ur had rebelled, and the destruction of Hammurabi's war memorial must have been an act of defiance on the part of the citizens ; within twelve months, in the year 1885 B.C., so nearly as we can reckon it, the Babylonian troops burst into the city, looted Nin-Gal's temple, flinging away what it was not worth their while to carry off, and set it on fire : the challenge and its punishment were clearly written in the ruins.

It was not only the temple of Nin-Gal that suffered from the fury of the troops of Babylon ; just outside the limits of the Sacred Area we excavated a section of the town proper, the residential quarter, and this too showed by its scorched walls and ash-covered floors that it had been overtaken at the same time by a like fate. It was one of the oldest parts of the city, where for many hundreds of years houses had been built and fallen into decay, only to pile up a platform for fresh building, so that by 2000 B.C. it was a hill rising high above the plain. Now the slopes were cut into terraces, and the houses of the time of Abraham stood on varying levels stepped down from the mound's summit to the flat ground below ; when they were destroyed the uppermost might suffer severely, but those on the lower terraces were deeply buried by the rubbish fallen from above, and many were so well preserved that it was easy to picture them as having been deserted but yesterday instead of thirty-eight centuries ago.

The illusion was greatly helped by the method of digging which we adopted here, for instead of digging down from the top we dug from the bottom upwards. At the outset we encountered, high up,

PLATE XI

(a) The memorial stones of Bur-Sin in the Moon-goddess's temple.

(b) The court-yard of the Moon-goddess's temple (in the centre, the brick base for Hammurabi's war memorial).

PLATE XII

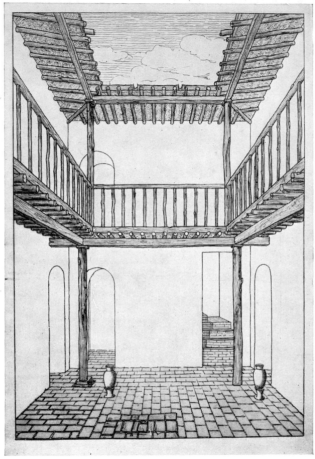

Restoration of a house of the time of Abraham.

buildings of a later date, and being unwilling to destroy these without the justification of further discoveries awaiting us underneath, I made the workmen go down in certain spots between the walls of the late buildings to sound the deeper levels ; 10 or 12 feet down we encountered walls which were built of burnt brick below—anything from five to fifteen courses of good brickwork set in mud mortar—and above of crude mud brick. These were good stout walls 2 feet thick ; but whereas the burnt-brick footings were as true as when they were first built, the superstructure of mud brick had often been pushed out of the straight by the weight of the later buildings on top of them, and, since they no longer presented a vertical face, would be extremely difficult to trace if one came upon them from above. The workmen therefore were ordered to work at the bottom of their pits, following the burnt brick first, and only when its direction was certain clearing away the overhanging earth and exposing the face of the mud brick ; where the mud brick had perished, as was often the case, the street or room was cleared, but the earth was left resting on the top of the burnt brickwork and gave the appearance of the wall which no longer existed. This, as I said, helped the illusion, but it was also an economical way of excavating,

L

as it minimised the quantity of soil to be removed, and where a wall of the later period coincided with one of the earlier there was no need to destroy it in order to explore the earlier levels.

The houses excavated were private houses of middle-class rather than of wealthy citizens ; they were of different sizes, and their ground-plan varied according to the exigencies of the available space and the means of the owner ; but on the whole they conformed to one general plan. They had been plundered and burnt in 1885 B.C., and they had been built at any time between that date and 2100 B.C., most of them having been more than once restored or reconstructed, so that they gave quite definitely the type of dwelling belonging to a representative class during a fixed period (Plates XII and XIII *a*).

Judging from the private houses of the age of Nebuchadnezzar which had been excavated by the Germans at Babylon, we had expected to find very modest dwellings one storey high and built of mud brick consisting of three or four rooms opening on to a court : instead of this we discovered that in Abraham's time men lived in houses built with walls of burnt brick below, rising in mud brick above, plaster and whitewash hiding the change in material,

two storeys high, and containing as many as thirteen
or fourteen rooms round a central paved court which
supplied light and air to the house. The streets were
narrow, winding, and unpaved, with on either side
blank walls unbroken by any windows, streets such
as one sees in any modern native town, impossible
for wheeled traffic. Against one house a mounting-
block showed that donkeys would be used for riding
or for freight, and the corners of the narrow lanes
were carefully rounded off to prevent injury to goods
or riders.

Through the front door of a house one passed into
a tiny lobby with a drain in its floor where the visitor
might wash his hands or feet, and from that into the
central court. On one side rose the brick stairs leading to the upper floor, and behind the stairs was a
lavatory with its terra-cotta drain ; then came the
kitchen, distinguished by its fireplace and the stone
grinders left on the ground ; a reception-room with
two doors or one door unusually wide was for guests,
another room might be for the servants, and yet
another the domestic chapel. Though the walls
stood in some places as much as 10 feet high, there
was no sign of ceiling-beams, so the ground-floor
rooms must have been lofty, a great advantage in this
hot climate. Of the upper floor nothing remained,

and its existence had to be deduced from such evidence as was available.

In the first place, there was the staircase. It is true that the stairs might lead only to a flat roof, but it seemed unlikely that so much of the restricted ground-space would be sacrificed to stairs serving no better purpose than that ; the late houses at Babylon had flat roofs, but the only approach to them was by outside ladders, not by solid stairs ; moreover, the use of the rooms on the ground-floor was tolerably certain, and there was no accommodation left for the family—there must therefore have been rooms above reserved for their living-quarters. The walls, internal and external alike, were so solid that it was natural to suppose that all rose to the full height of the house, so that the rooms above would duplicate those of the ground-floor, and in that case the access to them had to be considered. Below, all the chambers opened on to the court ; above, a passage running round would have made the rooms impossibly small even if the floors would have stood the weight of a cross wall, which was unlikely, so that either they all opened out of each other or there was some other method of approach.

In the middle of each courtyard there was a drain to carry off water, and in one case part of the pavement had got into disrepair and a square patch of bricks had been laid round the drain-head on the top of the old pavement ; this meant that the centre of the court was higher than the pavement nearer the walls, and water spilt on that surrounding part could never get to the drain, which therefore could not be intended to drain the court. Now, the roof of the house would be nearly flat, but sloping slightly inwards so as to carry off the rain-water, which would fall into the court, and its area was great enough for any ordinary storm to flood the court at once unless there were ready means of escape ; the water could escape only if it fell not close to the house walls, but directly on to the raised pavement in which the drain was, and for this to be possible the roof had to project over the court considerably beyond the wall line. If this were so, the part of the yard which could not be drained would never get seriously wet. If the roof projected so much, it was presumably to shelter something, and the only possible thing was a gallery running round the court and giving access from the stair-head to the upper rooms, whose doors in that case would correspond exactly to the doors on the ground-floor.

Examining the pavement carefully, we found that a single brick which was lying on it towards one

corner was not there by accident but was bedded
firmly in clay, and round it were remains of carbon-
ised wood. The argument from this was clear. If
the roof projected and if there were beneath it a
gallery, there must have been corner posts for its
support : given the character of the normal Eastern
carpenter, one at least of the posts would be too
short and would have to be jacked up on a brick or
stone, and the brick actually found would be such a
pole-rest and the burnt wood represented the pole.
Restoring three other poles in corresponding places
at the other corners, we found that we had a wooden
gallery just 3 feet wide whose supports were con-
veniently arranged not to block any of the ground-
floor doors. The staircase opened on to this, and by
its means one could go round to any of the upper
rooms without passing through the others. An omen
quoted on a contemporary tablet states that ' rooms
opening out of each other are unlucky, but those
opening on to the court bring good luck,' and our
restoration exactly fulfilled the requirements of
superstition as well as of convenience.

We must revise considerably our ideas of the
Hebrew patriarch when we learn that his earlier
years were spent in such sophisticated surroundings;
he was the citizen of a great city and inherited the

traditions of an ancient and highly organised civilisation. The houses themselves bespoke comfort and even luxury. Apart from the actual fabric there was little left to throw light on the daily life of the inhabitants, but one or two stores of tablets did bear witness to their intellectual interests. We found copies of the hymns which were used in the service of the temples, and with them mathematical tables ranging from plain sums in addition to formulæ for the extraction of square and cube roots, and other texts in which the writers had copied out the old building inscriptions extant in the city and had compiled in this way an abbreviated history of the principal temples.

And another illuminating discovery was that of the private chapels attached to the houses (Plate XIII*b*). At one end of the room the pavement would be raised by a single course of flooring-bricks, and on this there would be built against the back wall a brick altar ; above the altar or at one side of it there would be a shallow niche in the wall-face which was presumably intended for the sacred picture or clay figurines of the god, and against the side wall a square brick column of uncertain use; under the ' nave ' floor there would be a vaulted brick tomb in which each member of the family was laid when his

turn came to die. Not every house had a chapel,
and where there was none the family vault might lie
under any room, and sometimes beneath the floors
we found other single burials, the bodies set under
inverted clay coffins shaped like baths. It was the
custom that the dead man continued to inhabit the
house in which he had lived and his heirs dwelt
on in the rooms above his grave : the custom, barbarous as it may seem at first sight, accords with that
feeling of family continuity which is so strong, for
example, in the ancient Hebrews.

Occasionally we unearthed in the house ruins some
of the small clay figures of which very many examples
have been found in other parts of the residential site,
figures representing gods and their worshippers.
Sometimes they are rough models of the great temple
statues, sometimes they seem to be of a more inti-
mate sort ; but where the statues in stone or precious
metal have for the most part disappeared, these clay
copies afford invaluable material for the study of
contemporary art. They have a further interest in
that they are the *teraphim*, the household images
which Rachel stole from her father and Jacob buried
under an oak in Shechem. They may have formed
part of the furniture of the domestic chapels, and
certainly they illustrate that more personal side of

religion about which the texts concerned with the temple ritual have little or nothing to say.

One other aspect of life in the City of Abraham is brought into relief by our excavations. In the temple of Dublal-makh, about which more will be said later, there was found a hoard of many hundreds of tablets belonging to the business archives of the building. As king and landowner the god received rent and tithes and offerings of all sorts, and since there was no coined money, all these dues were paid in kind and required storage-room in the temple ; hence the need of the magazines which surround every sanctuary. The Sumerians were essentially business-like, and no transaction was recognised in law unless it was witnessed to by a written document, and so for all incomings the priests drew up formal receipts of which copies were filed in the temple archives ; whether it were a herd of sheep or a single cheese, a bale of wool or copper ore from foreign parts, the receipt was duly made out and entered. As the stores were drawn upon for the use of the temple, animals required for sacrifice, oil for squeaking door-hinges, wood for making a statue or gold for adorning it, the responsible official drew out an issue voucher giving the name of the recipient and his authority for the demand, and copies of these too were filed ; a great hoard of these such as we found in Dublal-makh throws no little light on the secular activities of a religious house.

Further there were on the temple premises regular factories where the raw materials paid as tribute were manufactured into finished goods, and we have elaborate balance-sheets of such a factory in which women attached to the service of the god were employed in spinning wool and weaving cloth, balance-sheets drawn up every month and three months with a nominal roll of the workers, and, in parallel columns, the amount of raw wool each had received, the tally of her work and its cost reckoned by the issues made to her of food and supplies. It is all very practical and curiously modern, and again we see how very different from what we might have thought were the antecedents of the Hebrew people.

Chapter VI

The Middle Age of Babylon

FROM THE TIME OF THE DESTRUCTION WROUGHT BY the Babylonians in 1885 B.C. darkness shrouds the city of Ur for nearly five hundred years. For the country as a whole it was not an exciting period ; a succession of kings who are little more than names sat on the throne of Babylon and added nothing to its history. At Ur not a single monument bears witness to any one of them ; so far as our excavations have gone, not one word of writing and not a brick in any of the buildings belongs to this stagnant age, and we can only suppose that the old buildings, patched up after the Babylonian inroad, were somehow sufficiently maintained not to make rebuilding imperative. At last, about 1400 B.C., there arose a king in Babylon, named Kuri-Galzu, who took an interest in the south country and thought it worth while to spend money in bricks and mortar : he started to repair the temples of the old Sumerian capital, but things had been allowed to go so far that his programme extended to a virtual reconstruction of at least the centre of the city.

The most striking monument of his that survives is the temple called Dublal-makh, the House of Tablets. Not far from the east corner of the

Ziggurat there was a little low mound which we could identify as one into which Taylor had dug seventy years before and had found in it a two-roomed brick building with arched doors which he took to be a small house of late date. We cleared of the clean drift-sand the two rooms which Taylor's workmen had roofed in with mats, so high did the walls stand, and had used as a shelter for themselves, and then proceeded to lay bare the outer face. Of the brick arches over the two side doors which Taylor had noted, one had since fallen, but the other remained intact, and the bricks of doorway and of walls, good burnt bricks laid in bitumen mortar, were freely stamped with Kuri-Galzu's name and proved that this was no late building but a temple of the fourteenth century before Christ. The arch was by a thousand years the oldest example of an arch standing complete above ground, and though we have since found other arches older by nearly two thousand years, yet when the discovery was made in the winter of 1924 we could hail it as one which revolutionised the history of architecture.

Two more discoveries followed. First we found that though the building of burnt brick consisted of two small rooms only, yet it had been added to at a later period with walls of mud brick which with their decoration of vertical grooves imitated the older work, from which, thanks to a coat of plaster and whitewash applied to the whole, they were indistinguishable : about this addition I shall speak later. Then we found that the brick pavement which extended in front of the building belonged to the later period only ; the walls of burnt brick went down deeper, and when we dug to their true ground-level this reached out only for 5 or 6 feet and then a fresh wall, grooved like that of the temple, dropped to a lower pavement. We followed this round and, cutting through the late brickwork and paved floor, exposed the original building, an isolated two-roomed shrine standing on a high pedestal which projected from the edge of the Ziggurat platform into a wide courtyard surrounded by high walls and chambers : this was the real Dublal-makh of Kuri-Galzu (Plate XIV *b*).

Of the little temple the antechamber was oblong in shape and had probably been vaulted ; the inner shrine was square and, judging from the exaggerated thickness of its walls, must have been roofed with a dome ; the outer door and that between the two rooms were unusually wide and their jambs were elaborately adorned with reveals, and since the smaller doors were arched it can safely be assumed that they were arched also. This would agree with the name of the building as inscribed on the bricks of the doorway ; instead of ' The House of Tablets ' we find here written 'The Great Gate' ; and when seven hundred and fifty years later the temple was restored by the Assyrians, it was the ' gate ' that was most emphasised. We found a door-socket of beautiful green stone bearing a long inscription, in which the governor of the city, after describing the dilapidation of the old building, boasts that he restored the Great Gate and set up doors of box-wood overlaid with brass, having silver hinges and lock-plates of gold. Why one and the same temple should possess two different names was not obvious until further excava- tions solved the problem in a very.interesting way.

Most of the brick pavement inside the ante-cham- ber had been destroyed by Taylor's workmen, and we therefore could dig down below floor-level with- out doing further damage. Just where the floor had been, the character of the bricks in the walls changed slightly, and stamped upon them was the name not of Kuri-Galzu but of a king of Isin who had reigned seven hundred years before him ; and the walls went down to the level of the outer court. Working on the outer face of the building where the pedestal had fallen away, we found that while the containing-wall of the latter was Kuri-Galzu's work, the filling consisted of broken bricks of the Isin period, and instead of running under the walls of the temple proper it only ran up against them ; in short, the pedestal was not what it appeared to be, a substructure on which the temple was built, but a skin masking the base of its walls ; and the masked portion was older than the superstructure.

Now things became clear. Kuri-Galzu had found the Isin temple ruinous and even its foundations giving away : he had razed the walls down to a height of about 6 feet from the ground, built a fresh wall round them, and had filled in the space between the old and new walls, and the interior of the chambers, so as to make one solid block ; then on the stumps of the old walls, now flush with his platform surface, he had built a temple which was an exact replica of its predecessor ; even the grooves on the wall-face reproduced the decoration of the time of the Isin king. But this older temple was not the first to occupy the site : under its walls we found others, rather differently aligned, stamped with the name of Bur-Sin, king of Ur in the Third Dynasty, and at the back was mud brickwork, part of it of the same Third Dynasty period—about 2220 B.C.—and part of it built in the herringbone

style with round-topped bricks and going back some
hundreds of years more to the Second Dynasty. The
Second Dynasty brickwork was a relic of the great
ring-wall which enclosed the Ziggurat terrace, and
since that line never altered, the back of Dublal-makh
was always flush with or embedded in the terrace wall.

Examining the temple again in the light of this
knowledge, we could see that its own back wall was
not original but an after-thought—it was a blocking
of what had once been an opening ; and the oldest
floor surviving in the sanctuary, that of Bur-Sin, was
not flat but was stepped up from the antechamber
so as to bridge the difference of levels between the
low-lying outer court and the Ziggurat terrace.
Originally the building had been the gateway of the
Ziggurat, 'The Great Gate.' The foundation-
inscription of Bur-Sin found on a door-socket
further helped us ; the building had been roofless
and ruinous, and he had repaired and covered it in
and had made it ' his Court of Justice, the net from
which the enemies of Bur-Sin shall not escape.'
That was the last clue required.

The original building was the gateway to the
Ziggurat, and since by it one passed on to holy
ground, the particular precinct of the Moon-god, it
was itself holy, and in the inner gatechamber there

PLATE XIII

(a) The house of the time of Abraham · photograph taken from the same point of view as the restored drawing.

(b) A domestic chapel, showing the altar and niche and the family vault below the broken floor of the nave.

PLATE XIV

(a) Clay figures from under the floor of a late building.

(b) The shrine Dublal-makh, showing Kuri-Galzu's platform.

would almost certainly be put a statue or an altar to which one could pay reverence on entering ; from a gate to a gateway shrine is but a natural transition. By the immemorial custom of the East the judge ' sits in the gate to give judgment,' and already by the time of Bur-Sin the Ziggurat gate had by its special sanctity come to be regarded as the king's supreme court. A remodelling of the Ziggurat platform and the making of a new entrance to it did away with the *raison d'être* of Dublal-makh, and the door to the terrace was blocked up and the building became simply a two-roomed temple.

But just as the name Ludgate has survived the walls of London, so tradition preserved the old name of the Great Gate, and even when Kuri-Galzu restored it in the fourteenth century B.C., this was the title inscribed by him on its door-jambs. The court still sat here, and its findings, written on clay tablets, were stored in the temple archives to be consulted in future cases, and from the new pedestal, standing under the huge arched doorway with the statue of the god in his shrine visible in the background as the inspirer and ratifier of judgment, the judges would pronounce their sentence to the crowd assembled in the broad paved court below.

Nearly always the inscriptions of Kuri-Galzu begin

M

with a set formula, ' that which was fallen down and of old time ruined from its foundations he has rebuilt,' making no claim to originality. He restored Dublal-makh, he restored the great temple of Nannar, as has been described, and the smaller temple of Nannar and his wife, the building called E-Nun-makh. There is only one striking exception to the rule. Of the temple of Nin-Gal set up by the royal priest Enannatum, the north-western half he did as usual restore, so far as the small temple in it was concerned, but the rest of the building was too ruinous and too deeply buried. Here he abandoned the old plan, and over the mounds covering the south-eastern temple set up houses for the lodging of the priests. But since Nin-Gal for some reason or other required twin shrines, Kuri-Galzu founded a new one inside the Ziggurat enclave on ground which had hitherto stood open, and here his inscriptions give him full credit as the first builder. It is interesting to see that here, where he had a free hand, the king adopts a plan unlike that of any of the older temples. There is an outer court with buildings round it, but the sanctuary complex, the temple proper, forms an isolated block, a small square compact building divided into a number of narrow chambers all once vaulted while over the central chamber rose a dome : it is exactly in the line of descent of modern Arab architecture.

Kuri-Galzu not only founded a temple here, but started a tradition. To unearth his building we had to dig through two temples of later dates set in the same place and dedicated to the same goddess. By 650 B.C. the Babylonian building was ruined and buried in its ruins, and the Assyrian governor who was commissioned to restore the sacred buildings of Ur had to start his work afresh and at a higher level. A hundred years later Nabonidus, last of the independent kings of Babylon, re-floored this temple and added to it a new and more imposing entrance, on the strength of such alterations claiming it as his own construction.

The reconstructed building was in a very ruinous state and contained few features of interest, but that of Sin-balatsu-ikbi the Assyrian proved more fruitful. One feature was distinctly novel. In the courtyard he dug a well, and in the lining of this and in the coping-wall put bricks bearing an astonishing variety of inscriptions. The temple was that of Nin-Gal, but in it there were side-chapels and altars and statues of many minor deities who formed the retinue of the great Moon-goddess, and as the well served all these alike, different bricks bore the name of each ; made ' for the throne ' of this god and ' for the

altar ' of that, a specimen of each had been inserted
in the wall of the well, and between them they gave
a remarkable idea of the catholicity of the worship in
a single temple.

When we came to pull up the bricks of the paving
we were surprised to find below them the foundation
cones, neatly-finished clay objects shaped like sugar-
cones and covered with cuneiform writing, standing
point upwards in the earth. From very early times
such cones had been employed, and always with a
certain change of fashion. Let into the sloping face
of the mud-brick wall which held up the terrace of
Ur-Nammu's Ziggurat, we had found quantities of
nail-like cones, the inscribed shaft buried in the
brickwork and only the rounded heads at regular
intervals making a sort of pattern on the wall-face—
and even they may have been hidden by a coat of
mud plaster. Where one of the Larsa kings had
built out from the same terrace a fort and postern-
gate, we found his cones not in the wall-face but
buried in its core, arranged in neat rows behind the
burnt-brick skin of the gate tower ; and these cones
were much larger than Ur-Nammu's, and instead of
the small nail-like head had a broad flat disk of clay
on which the inscription of the stem was repeated.
The Assyrian cones had no base at all and were placed

under the floor instead of in the walls ; in the following age barrel-shaped cylinders take the place of cones, and these are immured in the angles of the building.

In every case the inscription is hidden from sight, and it would seem that the intention of the king is not to parade his achievements before his fellow-men, but to keep the record of his piety fresh in the mind of the god, who presumably can see through a brick wall ; and probably there was, if not originally, at least as time went on, a second purpose. Everyone knew that the temple which the king built ' for his life ' could not last for ever, but that its crumbling walls would one day have to be restored by another ; if that later ruler discovered in the ruins the record of the first founder, he would in all likelihood respect it and even perpetuate it in his own inscriptions, and so his new building would acquire merit for the old king. This is what actually happened in a land where the continuity of tradition was so prized. In the very latest times, when Nabonidus repaired the Ziggurat he was careful to give full credit for its founding to Ur-Nammu and his son, and he has left on record the delight that he felt when deep in the foundations of an ancient temple which he was repairing he unearthed the foundation-tablet of Naram-Sin, son of

Sargon of Akkad, and looked upon that ' which fo three [*sic*] thousand years no human eye had seen.'

One can sympathise with Nabonidus's archæological enthusiasm; we had found plenty of Ur-Nammu cones scattered loose in the soil, but when for the first time we pulled one out from the mud-brick wall and saw on its stem the writing which had been deliberately hidden there more than four thousand years before, we experienced quite a different sensation, and though the cones of the Assyrian governor were set merely in the soil below the pavement, not bedded in brick-work, it was with a certain hesitation that we lifted them from the spot where the builders had placed them.

As we dug away the remains of Sin-balatsu-ikbi's temple we found evidence again of the piety which respects an ancient record. Lying together close to the foundations were four tablets, two of copper and two of stone, inscribed with the dedication of a building by Kuri-Galzu. They must have been found in the course of some work of demolition, perhaps of a temple which was not to be rebuilt on the old model or on the old site. Useless now and of no intrinsic value, they had been given careful reburial in the temple precincts with the idea, so it seems to me, that they might still bear witness before the gods to the merits of the dead king of Babylon, enduring after his works had perished.

Chapter VII

Nebuchadnezzar and the Last Days of Ur

SHORTLY BEFORE 600 B.C. NEBUCHADNEZZAR KING OF Babylon succeeded to the empire which Assyria had won. Of all the rulers of Mesopotamia he was perhaps the most indefatigable builder, and in almost every city of his dominions there are monuments witnessing to his passion for bricks and mortar : he rebuilt his çapital so thoroughly that modern excavators could find scarcely any trace of buildings older than his time—' is not this great Babylon, that I have built for the house of the kingdom by the might of my power, and for the honour of my majesty ? '—and at Ur practically the whole centre of the city, certainly the whole of the great complex of religious buildings which made up the Sacred Area, is overlaid with his restorations. Probably this was policy ; the new works would convince men of the might of his power, but further by showing his interest in the old Sumerian cities and his piety towards their traditional shrines he might win the support of the South Country and so secure himself against the discontent of the northern Assyrians whose sovereignty he had abolished. In the same way we may imagine that the building programme of

his grandson Nabonidus was not wholly uncon-
nected with the growing danger which threatened
his kingdom from the Persian uplands.

But Nebuchadnezzar did not confine himself to
restoration ; he was far more original than most of
his predecessors, and even when dealing with an old
building was ready to disregard old traditions. One
thing he did which was entirely new. The old
Sacred Area had consisted of religious foundations of
all sorts grouped together and in theory forming a
unity, but the unity was ill-defined ; sometimes the
outer walls of adjacent temples were continuous,
sometimes the buildings were more loosely disposed,
and it would seem that in fact the Sacred Area in
many places merged imperceptibly into the lay
quarters of the town. Nebuchadnezzar reformed all
this. A space 400 yards long and 200 yards wide was
marked out, a rough rectangle which enclosed all the
important buildings of Nannar's enclave, and round
this was built a wall of mud brick. It was a double
wall with chambers in the middle of it, the flat roofs
of which would make a broad passage along the wall-
top available for the manœuvring of troops in its
defence ; it was 33 feet wide and probably about
30 feet high, the face of it was decorated with the
double vertical grooves which were traditional for

temple walls (Plate XV *a*), and it was pierced by
gateways of which six have been discovered ; the
main gate, with a high gate-tower set back in a deep
recess, led immediately to the entrance of Nannar's
chief temple.

Parts of this great Temenos Wall are well preserved
and stand 6 feet high and more, and in other parts
where it ran over high ground and was therefore
more exposed it was difficult to trace it. We have
not dug it right out all the way round—that would
teach us no more than we know and would only
mean the total destruction of the mud brick by rain
and wind—but having excavated carefully certain
sections, we traced the rest by means of shallow
trenches which revealed only the upper courses, and
so were able to complete the entire circuit of the
Temenos in eight days. Sometimes in the course
of tracing we were temporarily baffled by unex-
pected changes of direction, and it is indeed difficult
to explain the minor irregularities in the line taken
by the wall. In places, where the back of an old
temple projected outside the area pegged out, it
has been ruthlessly cut away, and the wall of
enclosure makes the new back wall of the building ;
elsewhere the line is deflected as if to enclose some
monument which had to be respected, but as only

too often the denudation of the surface has resulted
in the complete disappearance of the monument we
cannot accept the explanation as certain.

Possibly there was a simpler reason. Examination
of the wall proves that it was built by various
gangs of workmen each having its own section,
and the collaboration between them was not very
good in that the foundations of adjoining sections
are laid at different levels and the projecting footings
are not continuous ; the irregularities of line may
be due merely to faulty methods.

But the Temenos Wall was an imposing structure,
and with its completion the Sacred Area took on a
new character ; it was much more a place set apart
than it had been in the past. And inside the wall
nearly everything bore the stamp of Nebuchadnezzar's creation. To-day over a good half of the
enclosure the weathering of the mounds has left no
vestige of the Late Babylonian buildings, and in
other places there may remain no more than such
scarcely intelligible wreckage as I described in
connection with the clay figures of guardian gods
found under the pavement ; but from what survives one can safely argue that Nebuchadnezzar
left very little untouched. We have seen that he
remodelled the great temple of Nannar and raised

the level of its outer court ; a description of the temple called E-Nun-makh will illustrate his radical treatment of old buildings.

The very first building which we excavated at Ur was E-Nun-makh. A low hillock rising close to the Ziggurat mound seemed to promise good results, and a trench driven into its flank at once produced walls of burnt brick enclosing paved chambers. It was a small square five-roomed building ; the door led into an antechamber, against the back wall of which, facing the entrance, was a brick base for a statue, and four doors, two in the back wall and one at either end, gave access to the other rooms which ran back the depth of the building. The two inner rooms were an exact pair ; each had a bench near the door and was divided into two parts by a screen in the farther part there was a brick altar against the wall and in front of it a brick table ; obviously each was a shrine for religious services. The two outer rooms were also a pair, but here there were no particular features to show their use. The duplicating of the arrangements in the temple was explained by the inscriptions on the bricks : it was the common shrine of Nannar and his consort Nin-Gal, and in it each deity had his or her special sanctuary.

In front of the building stretched a brick pavement

half enclosed by two projecting wings which had
been added in mud brick to the original square of
the shrine ; immediately in front of the door stood
an oblong brick altar for offerings, and to one side
remains of a second and larger altar from which a
covered drain led right across in front of the temple
door to some exit beyond the court ; the pavement
extended only to the line of the frontage of the mud-
brick wings and was then stepped down to a lower
level and continued to a boundary-wall which
separated it from the Sacred Way running through
the Sacred Area (Plate XV *b*).

The bricks of the pavement bore no stamp of
authorship, but their size and character proved them
to be Persian, belonging to the very latest date in the
history of Ur, and as a gate in the Temenos Wall
close by had been restored by Cyrus the Great, we
can probably attribute to him the last reconstruction
of the temple also. It was interesting to observe
that the position of the building and the details of
its arrangement agreed almost exactly with the description which Herodotus gives of the great temple
at Babylon in Persian times, but subsequent discoveries were to prove more interesting still.

It was clear that though the floors were Persian
the walls of the shrine were very much older ; in the

outer court there was an earlier pavement visible
where the new had been broken through, and the
same might be true of the chambers also. The order
was given to test this by pulling up twelve bricks in
one of the sanctuaries and digging down beneath
them. Our Arabs, who were new to the work, and
had always been told that on no account must they
disturb any brick that was in place, could not under-
stand this sudden sacrilege, and when they found
the order was serious jumped to the conclusion that
we were looking for buried gold, nor would they
believe me when I said that what we wanted was a
second brick pavement. I went off, leaving the men
at work, but within a few minutes one of them came
running to fetch me. 'We have found the gold!' he
said, and sure enough just below the paving-slabs
there was a whole treasure of gold beads and ear-
rings and pendants and one long gold pin topped
with a little figure of a woman wearing a long dress.
It might have been a votive deposit ; more probably
the things had been buried there for safety in some
moment of peril and had been forgotten. Nothing
of the kind was found anywhere else in the room or
in the other rooms of the temple, and nothing would
convince the Arabs that we had chosen to lift those
twelve bricks without knowing what lay beneath them.

Fortunately the second pavement was there as well as the gold, and about one in every four of its bricks bore the long stamp of Nebuchadnezzar, and this lower floor reproduced in every particular that of the Persian period : there were the same benches, altars, and tables, and in the court outside the same altar in front of the door ; only the second altar and the drain were missing, but the level between the wings of the building dropped as before to the wide outer court which reached to the temple walls.

The outer court was in bad condition, much of the pavement gone, and what remained curiously irregular, all in ridges and hollows. The reason for this was obvious from the outset and was proved as the work was carried down deeper : it had been laid over a series of chambers, and where the floor rested on the wall-tops it kept its level and where it had beneath it only the rubbish with which the old rooms were filled it had sunk or broken up altogether (Plate XV*b*). In the upper courses of the walls we found brick-stamps of Kuri-Galzu, and his socket-stones were in position by the doors, but fairly high up in the rubbish; in 1400 B.C., therefore, the rooms had been in use and had been restored with mud floors which lay only a very little below the pavement of Nebuchadnezzar, but they had been built earlier than that.

Lower in the walls came bricks of one of the Larsa kings (his floor had vanished), showing a previous reconstruction ; and then we found, mixed with the rubbish filling of the chambers, innumerable fragments of stone vases, some of them bearing inscriptions with the names of kings going back almost as early as the time of Sargon of Akkad (his own son was amongst them) and coming down to the close of the Third Dynasty of Ur. The vases belonged to a temple treasury and must have been broken up when Ur was sacked by an enemy, and judging from the dates given by the inscriptions, the occasion would have been the Elamite disaster which brought to an end the Third Dynasty, when the city of Ur was looted and burnt ; afterwards the scattered fragments of the sacred vessels must have been gathered up by some pious person and given decent burial under the new floor of E-Nun-makh.

Still the walls went down, and now we found on their bricks the stamp of Bur-Sin, king of the Third Dynasty, and below them mud bricks which we should scarcely have been able to identify but for the fact that in one place there was a vertical drain running through the wall to carry off rain-water from the roof, and this was constructed with burnt bricks and bitumen and bore the name of Ur-

Nammu, the founder of the royal house : he had built the temple in mud brick and his grandson had rebuilt it in more lasting material. Nor was Ur-Nammu the first to build : under his walls there were broken fragments of a construction in the round-topped mud bricks of an earlier day, and under these again walls of a yet more primitive description, built with what one could scarcely call bricks at all, so shapeless were they, mere lumps of clay which had been brought still damp and soft and set in clay mortar hardly to be distinguished from themselves, so that the whole ' green-walling ' structure, as our Arabs named it, having seen like rude work in modern times, became a homogeneous mass resembling *terre pisée* rather than a builded wall.

The temple was indefinitely old. Too little was left of the earliest building to show its form, but from the days of Ur-Nammu at least up to and after those of Kuri-Galzu, that is for more than a thousand years, successive builders had respected and repeated its ground-plan. The small five-chambered sanctuary was a thing apart ; it lay at the back of the building and was reached only by a passage which ran round three of its sides ; on the other side of the passage there were store-rooms and priests' chambers occupying the whole of the rest

PLATE XV

(a) The face of the great Temenos Wall of Nebuchadnezzar.

(b) The temple of E-Nun-makh. The part of the building
as remodelled by Nebuchadnezzar, showing the altar in
part of the sanctuary door, the pavement of the upper
court and, in the corner, one of Kuri-Galzu's chambers
underlying the broken floor of the lower court.

PLATE XVI

(*a*) A Kassite boundary-stone from Bel-Shalti-Nannar's museum.

(*b*) The clay 'label' from Bel-Shalti-Nannar's museum.

of the temple area and completely masking the sanctuary—it was hidden away and made as difficult of access as might be. I have said that the sanctuary rooms were very small and would hold but few people at a time ; taking this in conjunction with its inaccessibility, we are driven to conclude that E-Nunmakh was designed for a secret ritual such as might be fitting in what was really a harem temple, the special quarters of the god as married : only the priests would enter here and in privacy wait upon the twin deities.

This ancient tradition was completely set at naught by Nebuchadnezzar when he restored the temple. The rooms in front of the sanctuary, store-rooms and rooms which, as tablets found in them showed, were for the priestesses specially dedicated as concubines of the god who would naturally be at home in this harem building, were swept away ; the whole front of the sanctuary was opened up ; where the passage had been there was a raised pavement in the centre of which an altar rose, a statue-base was erected in the antechamber of the sanctuary facing its door, and where had been a maze of chambers the wide lower court afforded accommodation for a crowd of spectators. In the old temple everything had been secret ; now a numerous

N

public could watch the priest making his offerings on the open-air altar and behind him could see through the dim sanctuary's open door the image of the god.

There is no doubt that the remodelling of the building implies such a change of ritual, but how can this itself be explained ? The answer is given by the Old Testament story of the Three Children in the Book of Daniel. However miraculous a tale may be, its setting must have a certain verisimilitude, must contain some element of truth. Now, the gist of the story is this, that Nebuchadnezzar made a great image and set it up in a public place and ordered that at a given signal everybody was to fall down and worship it ; the Jews, who seem to have lived hitherto undisturbed in the land of their captivity, were by this order given the choice between idolatry and disobedience involving death. What was there new in the king's act ? Not the setting up of a statue, because each king in turn had done the same ; the novelty was the command for general worship by the public : for a ritual performed by priests the king is substituting a form of congregational worship which all his subjects are obliged to attend. So striking is the correspondence between the written story and the facts of the ruins and so completely do they explain each other that we must needs accept the background of the legend as historical. The alterations in E-Nun-makh were designed deliberately with a view to the religious reform attributed to its builder by the Old Testament.

Another old building was to undergo in these latter days a transformation not less radical. I have described Dublal-makh and its many vicissitudes down to the time when the Assyrian governor in 650 B.C. made its gates splendid with silver and gold; what I did not say was that in spite of his boasts the governor carried out most of his restorations with very poor material—the walls were of crude mud brick and the floor of beaten mud—and that what he did soon fell into disrepair. A hundred years later the work was again taken in hand by Nabonidus, the last of the Babylonian kings, and when we excavated the site his were the buildings which we first encountered.

In 550 B.C. nearly 8 feet of accumulated rubbish buried the court and surrounding chambers of the old temple, and no attempt was made by Nabonidus's workmen to clear them; instead the ground was levelled and new buildings were erected without any reference to what lay below : only the two-roomed shrine, the real Dublal-makh, raised high on the pedestal which had been built round it 850 years before, still stood above ground and could be incorporated in the new temple. On either side of the shrine new rooms were added whose walls, decorated with vertical grooves and covered with plaster and whitewash, could not be distinguished from the old ; one of these was a kitchen, one a room for ablutions with a bench for washing-basins and a drain, and one, with a doorway as imposing as that of the original shrine, must have been a second sanctuary. Flush with the threshold of the great gate there extended a large open court paved with brick and surrounded by buildings. Those which actually fronted on the court opened on to it and did not communicate with each other ; they were for the most part fairly large, and one would judge them to be intended for the official business of the temple. But facing the sanctuary entrance at the far end of the courtyard was a wide gateway from which a passage led right through to the rear of the building, and opening off this there were small complexes, each consisting of an open court with chambers along one or two sides of it, which were manifestly separate private residences, though as all lay within the heavy enclosure wall of the temple they were an essential part of the latter. To explain this there were brick inscriptions in plenty. Nabonidus was the builder ; the building was dedicated to the Moon-goddess ; it was a nunnery for the priestesses attached to the worship of Nannar and his spouse.

Now, from the inscriptions found seventy years ago by Taylor, we know that Nabonidus installed as High Priestess at Ur his own daughter, giving her much good advice as to her conduct in the post, and his new building, the E-gig-par as he called it, was to be her house. The old sanctuary of Dublal-makh presumably served as a sort of private chapel for the sisterhood, who, or at least the principal of them, were lodged in the separate quarters at the far end of the building, and the largest of these may well have been reserved for the princess herself, Bel-Shalti-Nannar, the sister of that Belshazzar who is notorious in Bible story.

The nunnery was interesting not only for its plan and associations, but also for its contents. In front of one of the side doors of the antechamber of Dublal-makh there lay a round-topped limestone relief on which was represented the god Ea, patron deity of the ancient city of Eridu whose ruins break the line of the horizon some twelve miles to the south-west of Ur. According to the old Sumerian convention the god is shown holding a vase from which two streams of water are pouring to the ground, while fish are swimming up and down in the streams ; as lord of the Waters of the Abyss Ea holds the source from which rise the twin rivers Tigris and Euphrates, givers of life to the land of Mesopotamia. The relief may have decorated the space above the door, but if so it was re-used, for it has nothing really to do with this Late Babylonian building but is a product of the great art of the Third Dynasty : how an object seventeen hundred years older than the nunnery came to be lying on its threshold will become evident from what follows.

Another object, found this time by the door of the kitchen which Nabonidus added to the sanctuary, was certainly of contemporary date, but it again was a stranger to its surroundings. Crushed together under a fallen brick we found at least a hundred slithers of ivory, many of them minute in size and as thin as tissue-paper, the ivory having rotted and split into its natural laminations : so delicate were they that they had to be hardened with celluloid before they could be picked up from the ground. When put together, the fragments took shape as a circular toilet-box decorated with figures of dancing girls carved on it in relief ; Egyptian rather than Oriental in style, the row of maidens hold hands and make a ring around the casket. This box was never made in Mesopotamia ; it is the work of one of those Phœnician craftsmen of Sidon or of Tyre whose skill in ivory-carving had made them famous throughout the Mediterranean world ; as an imported object it must have been a thing of price—indeed, that it was valued is clear, for it had been broken and riveted in antiquity—and possibly it belonged to the princess Bel-Shalti-Nannar herself.

But it was when we were clearing the surroundings of the courtyard that the discovery was made which most threw light on the character of the king's daughter. In a very much ruined room whose mud-brick walls rose scarcely above pavement level, one of the rooms fronting on the court which we had taken to be the business offices of the temple, we found a number of clay tablets of what are called the ' school exercise ' type ; they are flat disks of clay used for the teaching of writing. On one side the master inscribed his ' fair copy,' some easy sentence often taken from a well-known text, and the tablet was then handed to the scholar, who, after studying it, turned it over and on the back tried to reproduce what he had read ; sometimes the copy is very faulty and sometimes the boy has made a second attempt on the same tablet. We found a number

of these, and with them broken fragments of other
' school ' texts, bits of syllabaries giving columns
of words all beginning with the same syllable, much
like an old-fashioned English spelling-book, and one
fragment of a dictionary on which was an endorse-
ment ' the property of the boys' class.' Here was
definite proof that the priestesses kept a school on
their premises.

And a still more up-to-date touch was given by the
contents of the next room. The pavement was very
close to the modern surface, which was terribly
denuded by weather, and not more than a foot of
loose rubbish covered the brickwork ; there seemed
little hope of finding anything in such a spot. But
suddenly the workmen brought to light a large oval-
topped black stone (Plate XVI *a*) whose top was
covered with carvings in relief and its sides with
inscriptions ; it was a boundary-stone recording the
position and the outlines of a landed property, with
a statement as to how it came legally into the
owner's hands and a terrific curse on whosoever
should remove his neighbour's landmark or deface
or destroy the record. Now, this stone belonged
to the Kassite period of about 1400 B.C. Almost
touching it was a fragment of a diorite statue, a
bit of the arm of a human figure on which was an

inscription, and the fragment had been carefully trimmed so as to make it look neat and to preserve the writing ; and the name on the statue was that of Dungi, who was king of Ur in 2280 B.C. Then came a clay foundation-cone of a Larsa king of about 2000 B.C., then a few clay tablets of about the same date, and a large votive stone mace-head which was uninscribed but may well have been more ancient by five hundred years.

What were we to think ? Here were half a dozen diverse objects found lying on an unbroken brick pavement of the sixth century B.C., yet the newest of them was seven hundred years older than the pavement and the earliest perhaps two thousand : the evidence was altogether against their having got there by accident, and the trimming of the statue-inscription had a curious air of purpose.

Then we found the key. A little way apart lay a small drum-shaped clay object (Plate XVI *b*) on which were four columns of writing ; the first three columns were in the old Sumerian language, and the contents of one at least were familiar to us, for we had found it on bricks of Bur-Sin, king of Ur in 2220 B.C., and the other two were fairly similar ; the fourth column was in the late Semitic speech. ' These,' it said, ' are copies from bricks found in the ruins of Ur, the work of Bur-Sin king of Ur, which while searching for the ground-plan [of the temple] the Governor of Ur found, and I saw and wrote out for the marvel of beholders.' The scribe, alas ! was not so learned as he wished to appear, for his copies are so full of blunders as to be almost unintelligible, but he had doubtless done his best, and he certainly had given us the explanation we wanted. The room was a museum of local antiquities maintained by the princess Bel-Shalti-Nannar (who in this took after her father, a keen archæologist), and in the collection was this clay drum, the earliest museum label known, drawn up a hundred years before and kept, presumably together with the original bricks, as a record of the first scientific excavations at Ur.

Before long the storm which had long been gathering in the East burst. Belshazzar, who had been acting as regent for his father and commanded the troops in the field, was defeated and killed by the invading Persian army ; Nabonidus was taken prisoner when Babylon fell, and his dominions passed into the hands of Cyrus the Great. Cyrus seems to have paved the way for his armed attack by a campaign of scurrilous propaganda directed against the person and character of the late king, and after his victory he took a particular pleasure in defacing his monuments ; at Ur the ruinous state of Naboni-dus's buildings is often manifestly due to wilful vandalism. But the conqueror was not so secure on his newly-won throne that he could afford to flout the feelings of his subjects, and a definite policy of conciliation provided for the repair of the temples, even of those which had been desecrated as being memorials of the last independent king.

When we were tracing the course of the great Temenos Wall built by Nebuchadnezzar we found in one of the north-east gates the stone door-sockets in position in the brick boxes which kept the earth away from the hinge, and the bricks bore the in-scription of Cyrus ; the new ruler had repaired the circuit wall of Nannar's temple, and, as we have seen, it was almost certainly he who was responsible for the last restoration of E-Nun-makh, the joint shrine of Nannar and Nin-Gal. The inscription on the bricks has a familiar ring ; ' the great gods have delivered all the lands into my hand,' it begins, and we think of the proclamation of Cyrus in the Book of Ezra which also had to do with the restoration of a temple : ' The Lord God of Heaven hath given me all the kingdoms of the earth ; and he hath charged me to build him an house at Jerusalem, which is in

Judah.' That act of clemency, which to the captive Jews appeared miraculous, was an incident in a scheme applied to the whole kingdom : whether the god was Jehovah or Nannar mattered little to Cyrus ; his purpose was to placate his people by subsidising their particular forms of worship, and the temples of Ur gained a fresh lease of life from the catholic generosity of the Persian.

But the lease was a short one. The city had long since lost all political importance and deserved consideration only as a traditional centre of religious feeling in the South, and it was perhaps about this time that an event occurred which was to seal its doom for ever. In the old days the river Euphrates, or an important branch of the river, washed the walls of Ur on the west, and from it innumerable canals big and small led the water off into the fields which spread far across the plain, and up and down the main canals went the ships bringing trade from the Persian Gulf and from the other towns on the river-banks. To-day the Euphrates runs 10 miles to the east of the ruins and the great plain is a barren desert. When the river changed its course we do not yet know, but the drying-up of the old bed meant the stoppage of water-borne traffic, the ruin of the whole elaborate system of irrigation, and the end of agriculture ; there was not the energy or the capital for the installation of a new system, and the starving city had no longer any reason for existence. Gradually the inhabitants moved away to other homes, the houses crumbled, the winds sweeping across the now parched and desiccated levels brought clouds of sand which they dropped under the lee of the standing walls, and what had been a great city became a wilderness of brick-littered mounds rising from the waste.

It is very likely that the blow fell in the Persian period. After Cyrus no king's name appears on any brick to show that the government was at all interested in the buildings of the city ; on the contrary, all the evidence proves that neglect speedily brought them to ruin. In the rubbish heaps which covered the sanctuary of Nannar's great temple we found crooked walls ill built of old bricks collected from ruins of all dates ; they were mere huts without symmetry or plan, but under the foundations we discovered a clay jar containing tablets which proved that this was the last degenerate phase of the temple. Here a handful of priests lived on and eked out their existence on the tithes which a faithful few still brought to the dishonoured House of Nannar.

On the other side of the Ziggurat we unearthed, lying above the chambers built by Nabonidus for the service of Nin-Gal's temple, kilns set up by some Persian potter ; his ovens ran up almost against the side of the huge tower, and the ' wasters,' the pots damaged in the firing, and the little clay tripods which kept apart the plates piled in the kiln and prevented the glaze sticking them one to another, were mixed in the rubbish with the blue-glazed bricks fallen from the walls of the little shrine which was the Ziggurat's crowning glory. Here and there in the remains of Persian houses dated tablets have been found which carry on the history of the inhabited town to about the middle of the fifth century before Christ, and thereafter there is silence.

About this time the Persian kings definitely adopted the Zoroastrian creed, whose pure monotheism rejected the images and temples of idolatry, and very likely iconoclasm hastened at Ur the slower process of natural decay ; but that process of itself was sure. The populous city became a heap, its very name was forgotten ; in the holes of the Ziggurat owls made their nests and jackals found a hiding-place, and the Bedouin pitched their camps under the shelter of the ' Mound of Pitch,' little guessing that here had lived Abraham, the founder of the Jewish nation and of their own race, Ibrahim Khalil Abdurrahman, the Friend of God.

INDEX